REMEMBER *Eternity*

Great Is Thy Faithfulness

J. E. STARKS-BROWN

Remember Eternity: Great Is Thy Faithfulness

Copyright © 2022 by J.E.Starks-Brown

PB: ISBN: 978-1-63812-402-3
Ebook ISBN: 978-1-63812-403-0

All rights reserved. No part in this book may be produced and transmitted in any form or by any means, electronic, or mechanical, including photocopying, recording, or by any information storage and retrieval system, without permission in writing from the copyright owner.

The views expressed in this work are solely those of the author and do not necessarily reflect the views of the publisher hereby disclaims any responsibility for them. Published by Pen Culture Solutions 09/15/2022

Pen Culture Solutions
1-888-727-7204 (USA)
1-800-950-458 (Australia)
support@penculturesolutions.com

⇝ FOREWORD ⇜

In these perilous and uncertain times, there remains one undeniable fact that we all must face and that is Eternity. As we live our everyday lives, year in and year out, we are ever moving closer to the era where time will be an extinct entity. In our human natures, we tend to view Eternity as a fact that is eons away or something to be dealt with after we tend to our own temporal agendas.

The Word of God leaves no doubt about the two eternal destinations that we have the options to choose from. Eternal reward in Heaven or eternal damnation in Hell leaves no choice to the reasonable mind and this being said, it only makes sense to "Remember Eternity".

In this society, we are bombarded with countless winds of doctrine that have forms of godliness while denying the power thereof which is a danger to the eternal soul. Ephesians 4:5 (KJV) plainly states that there is One Lord, one faith, one baptism. This one Lord, Jesus Christ, commanded us in St. Matthew 28:19 to be baptized in the name of the Father (Jesus), the name of the Son (Jesus) and the name of the Holy Ghost (Jesus), not His titles. This was confirmed through the Apostle Peter on the Day of Pentecost (Acts 2:38), when three thousand souls were added on the Birth Day of the Church. The ingredients of genuine godly sorrow or repentance from sin, water baptism in the name of Jesus for the remission or removal of sin, coupled with the baptism of the Holy Ghost. The undeniable evidence of this second birth experience is the speaking in other tongues as the Spirit of God gives the utterance. There is no substitute for this awesome encounter with God that empowers the born again believer to overcome the sinful Adamic nature that we are all enter into this world with. It is not to be scoffed at or minimized by those who would downplay its significance or importance.

"Remember Eternity" opens with eighteen year old Janice Scott who impulsively leaves her home in Washington D.C. to join her cousins in Des Moines Iowa. While harboring a secret, she develops new relationships and begins to encounter situations that ultimately transform her from an angry and cynical teen-ager into a new creature in God. As one life touches another, circumstances evolve into a myriad of events that in time give God the glory for His wonderful works to the children of men.

Janice discovers the power of Agape' love through those that are Spirit filled while enduring several life changing hardships that forever change her perspective on life. Through these adversities, she begins to experience a father-daughter relationship that she was deprived of during her unstable childhood and this in turn enriches her spirit in a way that had been before unimaginable. Because of the God given wisdom and compassion of her surrogate father Douglas, she learns how to depend on the God of her salvation as she simultaneously begins to give of herself to others.

"Remember Eternity" is an intimate look into a family's struggles, victories, trials and tribulations of the righteous which are all a part of the sanctified set apart life that God is calling for in these troubling and stressful times.

~Introduction~

"Remember Eternity", as its title suggests, is a reminder to us all that there is a life beyond this one in which we now live. "It is a fictional, based on spiritual facts look into the lives of a not so ordinary spirit filled family, in the process of making preparations for Eternity.

Set in the present day city of Des Moines, Iowa, the intention of "Remember Eternity" is to emphasize the importance and power of relationships that have the ability to change the course of our lives. It is centered around the matriarchal figure of Frances Michaels, her three adult daughters, one son, their spouses and grandchildren. She is recognized as a spiritual symbol of wisdom and experience, ever nurturing, advising and whether solicited or no, her words are lovingly accepted with gratitude. Rooted and grounded in the life of holiness, she is full of rich testimonies of God's goodness in a stress filled world. As her young twenty something nieces Sheila and Ruth, along with high school senior " 'Nita" come into play, relationships flourish in the midst of adverse situations.

As the Remember Eternity series continues, this extended family will prosper and never cease to witness the faithfulness of God in a world that seems to have turned upside down. Michael and Janice will reap the benefits of "doing it God's way" in a society that mocks the tradition that God has ordained and honored. Spiritual prosperity will prevail after the suffering of the righteous proves and perfects those whom God has chosen to be His "very elect."

Many are the afflictions of the righteous: but the Lord delivereth him out of them all. [Psalms 34:19] [KJV].

Chapter 1

AUGUST 23
SUNDAY

"I don't know what it is about this house but Aunt Frances told me this is the third time that this has happened." Marie remarked with Chris and James out on the deck around nine o' clock.

"It's not the house but it's the spirit of the people in here that's makin' the difference." James said after a moment.

"She told me that if she hadn't been listenin' to what they were talkin' about out here, it wouldn't have happened like it did." She said, referring to Kathryn.

"I was out here when he was talkin' and I had never heard so much detail before either." James remarked. "I mean the way he broke it down, it almost felt like you were there and that was over twenty years ago."

"But when you're ready, it doesn't take a lot to get what you came for as they say." Chris remarked. "Did you take her home?"

"Michael and Janice did, I wanted to come back here for a minute before I go back." She said. "And right before we left church after she got baptized, she wanted me to tell you how much she loved bein' here today."

"That's a good thing, she won't ever forget this day either." James said. "And actually, I feel bad because she hasn't been comin' out here before now."

"I don't want you feelin' guilty because Janice had asked her about that right after we got her moved here but she wasn't feelin' it." Marie said. "Then after I found that note that she left, that's what set a fire under me to get here because it was really scary, you know what I mean?"

"You had to do what you had to do and if you hadn't, the outcome might've been altogether different." James told her.

"And I was tellin' Janice earlier when we were waitin' on her at church, that if she hadn't gotten on that plane back in February, and flew here on a dare from 'Nita, a whole lot of things would be different." She said, pausing. "And I've never really had the chance to thank both of you for what you've done for her."

"It was a little sticky at first because she wouldn't call Kathryn to let her know where she was." Chris recalled. "Then after we found out she was pregnant; we really didn't have a choice about things but it's all worked out." "She's been a lot of help to us and we'll probably really miss her when she's not here anymore."

"So, it'll be three babies in here by January huh?"

"That depends on what her and Michael do, she might not be here but if she is, we're okay with it." James said. "I made sure we have enough square feet."

"You really did, I almost got lost in there."

"And they're not gettin' any smaller so I was thinkin' ahead."

"Have you ever thought about startin' your own business?" She asked him.

"Someday maybe." "I would be takin' too much of a chance to do that right now."

"But you have thought about it, I can tell."

"Yeah I have but I'm in the middle of some stuff where I am and until it's settled, I'm not goin' anywhere."

"Is somebody tryin' to start some mess with you?"

"It takes Janice to really break it down and it might be affectin' my bottom line so it's somethin' that I have to deal with."

"Is it some racial stuff goin' on?"

"It probably is and that's why I'm not gonna let it move me out of there."

"So what's happenin'?" She persisted. "Does it have anything to do with Janice?"

"I think things were goin' on under the table before she started workin' there because of me." Chris spoke up. "Then when she got hired, there was some crazy stuff goin' on about who the baby's father is, just because they come and go at the same time."

"And it's all about the race card, whether they wanna admit it or not." James said. "But that's a hard thing to prove but some things you just know."

"Some things the Lord will let you know and you can't really put your finger on it but you're right, you just know."

"And this stuff didn't start until my original company was taken over by the elitist snobs that are in charge of the place now." James said as he felt a spirit of resentment and anger attempt to overcome him.

"Elitist snobs?" She said, repeating after him. "Wow, that's pretty messy right there."

"It is and when you're in a place where they cater to old money and millionaires, you're gonna get lost in the shuffle if you're not playin' that game."

"And you're not playin' that game huh?"

"I could but I can't go there and it's rubbin' certain people the wrong way which is where the fight comes in." He said. "If they can't get you out one way, they're gonna create somethin' else and that's where the subtil racism comes in."

"So they know that your wife isn't a white woman so they don't think you fit their profile." Marie said in a knowing manner.

"Exactly, you're gettin' it ma'am."

"But I know that you're one of the top guys that's bringin' in a lot of profit so doesn't that count for anything?" She asked. "And the only reason I know that is because of what Janice told me."

"How did that come up?"

"We were talkin' about how you laid this house out and she told me that you were in the top five designers in the place." She said. "And they're trippin' over somethin' that doesn't have anything to do with your job?"

"It's all about the image that you have and if you don't fit that criteria, you're pretty much behind an eight ball."

"But they don't know who they're messin' with, that's the thing you have to remember."

"I know that's right but in the mean time, it's a fight to keep myself in a place where the Lord can step in and do what He does." He answered. "There's not a day that goes by that I'm stoppin' myself from writin' a nasty e-mail that says to take this job and shove it but that's exactly what they want and I'm not goin' that way."

"You're not givin' them the satisfaction huh?"

"That's it so what I'm doin' is layin' low and actin' like it's all good because in a way, it is." He said. "I already know that this is gonna come out in my favor so I refuse to stress myself out about it."

"Sounds like faith to me but I guess when you've seen the Lord work like you did, you really don't have any reason to doubt God at all."

"And I have to keep tellin' myself that this is just helpin' me to get over my stuff that's not good for me to be hangin' on to." "I'm findin' out that they're not gonna change unless the Lord gets involved but that doesn't give me an excuse to be just as wrong as they are."

"Because we're without excuse huh?"

"You better believe it and this thing that we just went through with these babies got a lot of stuff out of me that didn't belong there,you know what I mean?"

"And that's what I've been wantin' to hear from you because it's one thing to see it on YouTube, but I need to hear it from you live." She said with anticipation.

"Basically what happened, I went to the doctor a little over a month ago, just for a routine first sonogram so we thought." Chris began.

"So you were there too?" She asked James.

"I was there and we weren't surprised when we found out that it was two because I knew the signs." Chris said . I was three months and looked like I was four or five so that wasn't that big of a deal." "But when I looked over at the screen and saw for myself that they were connected, I lost it." She said in retrospect. "I was so used to havin' all of these normal pregnancies with all these healthy babies and this was hittin' us like a ton of bricks."

" Didn't they tell you that you needed to go on and have 'em aborted?" Marie asked, recalling the Youtube video.

"Of course, that's the first place they wanna go but when they found out that we wasn't gonna do that, they just pretty much wrote me off as a hopeless case." "They were gonna die and that was the end of it."

"Or so they thought."

"Exactly." She continued. "And this is the strangest thing about the whole thing." "I got a phone call from a nurse practitioner a couple of days later and she told me that my doctor had taken another look at the sonogram and they found out that I have a bicornuate uterus." She said as she watched her puzzled reaction.

"Okay, you know you have to translate that don't you?"

"That's just the medical term for two wombs." James said.

"Are you serious?" Marie asked in amazement. "I didn't know there was a such thing."

"I didn't either and later on, after we found out that it's a boy and a girl, that explains why they're not identical." Chris further explained. "Their explanation is that after they were concieved, somehow they fused together and that's why they were callin' 'em conjoined." "It sounds crazy but like Douglas said after he found out about it."

"I can't wait to hear this."

"I told him first, then I talked to Jane about it." James began. "This wasn't that long after her mother got her help so I needed to talk to somebody that knew where I was comin' from." He continued. "But he told me the Lord was doin' one of two things." "Either they misdiagnosed it or the Lord allowed it to happen so we could see one more time that situations like this are a light thing when it comes to what God will do when you believe Him."

"Oh I love it." Marie said, shaking her head. "What did Aunt Frances say when she found out?"

"She said not to panic because God is in control and I lost it again but it was what we needed to hear." Chris admitted. "And we knew that but it helped to hear it anyway."

"Her and Douglas just kind of feed off each other don't they?"

"They do, that's a good way to put it because when they get together, stuff happens." James said.

"And this was a mess when you looked at it with your natural eyes I guess."

"It was, they said it defied all of the odds but there it was, they couldn't deny what they were lookin' at."

"And I was startin' to have these thoughts that it might be better if I would have a miscarriage and just be done with it." Chris said. "I went over to talk to Irene and Douglas about it and I felt better after I got that off my chest and I feel bad about it now but I was keepin' it real."

"You have to and there's no point in tryin' to act like you're strong when you're havin' a weak moment." Marie said. "And all of us know that the Lord knows what we're gonna think way before we do so what's the point?"

"There is no point and he told me that night not to be worried and fearful because that was a sure sign of doubt and mistrust about the power of God, and he was as serious as a heart attack as the kids say."

"Him and Aunt Frances do not play and I'll be glad when I get to the place where they are."

"And his testimony is even more powerful because of the way he used to be." Chris said. "He was horrible."

"So you remember when him and Irene were out there huh?"

"I do, I was probably fourteen or fifteen when she met him and they were seriously out there."

"And that's what makes it such a big thing when you see how the Lord uses him."

"You know it." Chris said, agreeing with her."Then one day, it was a Saturday afternoon, I just had to get away and I ended up at their house." "They stopped what they were doin' to sit and listen to me in the middle of my pity party."

"But Chris, I don't think I'd feel bad for feelin' like you were, that was some serious stuff to have to deal with." Marie remarked.

"It was but when I look back on it now, I really don't think the Lord was pleased with the way I just pretty much fell apart." "And Douglas told me somethin' that I won't ever forget that has helped me deal with other stuff."

"Here comes somethin' deep and profound." Marie said, laughing a little.

"It wasn't even somethin' that I didn't already know but he said that sometimes it takes a red hot test to let us know where we're not, and where we need to come up." "And that day, I had it so bad that he wouldn't let me drive home."

"Are you serious?"

"I was a hot mess and that was when he called James over there and told us some things that made a big difference." Chris said. "And it wasn't anything deep that he said but it helped to hear somebody else's thoughts about it."

"That was when he took authority over the whole thing and told me that it was time for me to heal my children." James said, quoting him."He actually took my hand and laid it right here." He added as he demonstrated to her what had happened.

"The man was serious huh?" Marie barely asked as her spirit bore witness to their testimony.

"I don't think I had ever seen him so passionate and deadly serious in my life Marie, I'm not kiddin.'" Chris said. "And after what we had just seen with Jane's mother, I think he felt like we were without excuse and we were."

"Oh my God, I had no idea." "All of these details weren't on the video and I'm just about in shock." Marie said then.

"But it's that kind of faith that causes God to move and this was on a Saturday that this happened." James said."And that Friday almost a week later, we really got our minds blown."

"I don't know if I can take any more." Marie said as she allowed herself to openly cry tears of joy for them.

"Yeah you can because it'll take your faith to another level if you really need to see the Lord do things for you." Chris told her. "So that happened on a Saturday and that Friday night, almost a week later, Patti shows up at Jane and Paul's over there to tell them about somethin' she saw in the chicken house over there." She said, glancing towards it.

"I think Janice told me somethin' about that but I need to hear it from you too."

"Douglas was over there talkin' to Jane and she knocked on their patio door." Chris began "She said she was shakin' a little bit and told them that another angel told her not to be afraid and to tell me that the baby was healed, long story short."

"I love that little girl because she has the faith that we're supposed to have and she's showin' us somethin'." Marie said. "And a lot of times, it takes kids to show us stuff that we wouldn't see otherwise, I love that in her."

"And since she's had the Holy Ghost, she's got this boldness that she didn't seem to have before." Chris remarked. "I heard her tell 'Nita the other day that she needed to get it right before Jesus comes back."

"Are you serious?" "What was her answer?" Marie asked, amused.

"She said she already knew that and she told her to pray for her."

"And when it's like that, I found out that's all you can do." "When I got back home in April, I tried to tell mother about what had happened to me and she looked at me like I was crazy because you just don't get it 'til it happens to you."

"But now she knows and you and Janice should have an easier time with her."

"I know we will but I just hope this doesn't make her feel like she's not gonna have problems anymore." Marie said. "I have a friend at church back in D.C. that made the mistake of thinkin' that her problems were gonna disappear because the Lord gave her the Holy Ghost one night."

"Not." Chris said. "Sometimes that's when some problems start, like with Irene and Douglas."

"Jerry didn't like it either and it took a minute for him to know that this was for the better."

"Is he still comin' next month?"

She nodded. "He'll be here on the sixth; he's stayin' with Donna and Randy and I'll probably end up over there dependin' on how well mother is, she might not even need me that much any more."

"Yes she does, don't leave her yet." Chris told her. "She's gonna need you to help her really understand what she has now, because the last thing you want is for her to slip back to the place where she was."

"That can't happen, she needs to be goin' to as many Sunday school and bible classes as she can to get her strength up."

"We'll make sure that happens, between all of us there's no reason why that won't be taken care of." Chris said. "And Jane told me that Florence can't wait to jump in and do what she can so that might be the answer to a lot of things right there."

"And when you think about it, that really is an interestin' combination." James said.

"It is but I know for sure that she was an answer to prayer and because of the way it went down, I don't have a problem with that at all." Marie said with confidence. "They're about the same age and I think they'd be good for each other so whatever creative ways they come up with, I'm all for it."

"Honey look in that cabinet next to the refrigerator and you'll find a box of tea and if you see anything else in there you might want, help yourself." Kathryn told Janice as she and Michael sat down at her kitchen table.

"I see stuff in here but I've already eaten enough for today, I'm not tryin' to gain too much more weight."

"Can you tell her that she doesn't have anything to worry about?" Kathryn asked Michael then as uncontrolled tears fell down her face.

"It's just too much right now huh?" He asked as he passed her a napkin.

"It really is, and I can't believe this is me after all of this time." She managed to say. "And you remind me so much of your brother."

"I get that a lot and I guess if I had a beard, we'd really be almost like twins huh?" He asked her as they gradually began to feel more at ease with one another.

He's a wonderful person and when I think about the way we started out, I could almost cry when I think about the way I acted." She said apologetically.

"But we've all done things that we aren't proud of but this is your new start and nobody is holdin' anything against you." Michael told her. "I don't think that's keepin' him awake at night so it's all good." He added as Janice sat down after she opened a text message from Craig's mother, Mary Ann Davis.

"What's up, what happened?" He asked as he read the expression on her face.

"She really didn't have to do this." She said after a moment as she showed him a picture of Craig in his casket before his funeral.

"What is it honey?" Kathryn asked her.

Without saying a word, Michael passed the phone over to her.

"Can you go and take care of her for me?" She asked him after looking at the picture and noticing her reaction. "I think I need to go be by myself for a while." She said as she slowly got up from her chair and headed towards her bedroom.

"I don't know whether she did this to hurt me or what but this just brings it all back Michael." Janice remarked five minutes later as they sat in her car. "I thought all of that was behind me and then she does somethin' crazy like this."

"It is behind you so don't let this bring you down baby." He gently told her. "Especially after what happened today."

She nodded a little as she stared at the picture again. "And I've never told anybody this before now but if I tell you, I might feel better." She added.

"Then let me have it as Douglas says." Michael said in an attempt to some how lift her mood.

"I'm sittin' here about to have this dude's baby that raped me." She managed to get out. "And I never told anybody that because it would sound like I was lyin'."

"You didn't think anybody would believe you?" Michael asked as he tried to hide his shock from her.

She nodded then. "And that's why I don't feel bad about this but I don't think that's right either." She admitted as they noticed Marie pull up next to them in the driveway.

"I just love the way the Lord does things." He said as he slowly opened the door and got out.

"Everything okay?" Marie asked him a minute later as she read the expression on his face.

"I've got to take a walk, I'll be back." He told her as he turned and headed towards the fountain in the middle of the village.

"What's goin' on honey?" Marie asked Janice as she got in the car with her. "Is mother okay?"

"Yeah she's good and I'm so glad for today because this is what I got from Craig's mother about ten minutes ago." She said while passing the phone to her.

"Are you serious?" "Really?" She commented a moment later after looking at the picture on the screen.

She nodded. "And as soon as I looked at that, it just all came back Marie." She said, close to tears.

"Did Michael see this?"

She nodded again. "Then I told him what really happened and maybe I shouldn't have but it's too late." She said, shrugging a little.

"How do you mean what really happened honey, you might as well get it out of your system because I can tell you're holdin' it back." She told her.

"He raped me and I haven't said anything because it would sound like I was lyin'." She explained with an air of anger mixed with a sense of relief that her hidden truth had finally come out, triggered by the image of her child's now deceased "father". "I asked him for a ride home from work on New Year's eve and I think he had been drinkin'." She continued as she recalled the awful experience. "He told me if I wanted a ride home that I would have to pay for it."

"You were at work??" Marie asked her, in shock.

She nodded. "He was closin' up and I was waitin' on him to get stuff done and he made me go in the men's restroom with him. She said as her tears began to flow. "He threw me down on the floor and told me if I wanted a ride home to shut up and let it happen and Marie it was my first time and it hurt so bad." She told her, holding nothing back as Marie reached over to hold and embrace her in an effort to calm her.

"Does it make you feel better that you got all of that out?" Marie asked her a minute later.

"It does and I had blocked all of that out but when I looked at this picture, it just brought it all back." She said as she got tissues out of the console between them.

"Then you know what honey?" She asked her.

"What?"

"It's up to you but if it was me, I would delete this and get my number changed so she won't be able to send you anything else." Marie suggested to her. "Then when the baby's born, I can take pictures and send 'em to her and that way she won't be able to keep doin' stuff like this."

"It's not that I want keep things from her but she didn't have to do this." Janice said. "And she looks just like him so it'll be almost like seein' him every day."

"Janice we're gonna take it one thing at a time so don't worry about things like that." "If she looks like him, it is what it is but that's not what's important right now." Marie gently told her. "Did you tell Michael everything that you just told me?"

"I just told him that he raped me and that's when he got out of the car after he saw you pull up."

"He said that he had to go for a walk and I'm gonna tell you why he reacted like that." Marie said, pausing. "I think that I know him well enough to say that he really does love you and the first thing he probably wanted to do was to show you how it's supposed to be done." "But he knows that's not an option right now because you're not his wife yet, you know what I mean?"

"So he had to walk away to stay out of trouble huh?"

"I mean we have to keep it real and all the devil wants is to see you two mess up." "But because you're doin' it God's way, he probably did what he had to do." Marie said. "He's lettin' his Holy Ghost work and I'm proud of both of you because it could've gone another way, believe me."

"But that's not why I told him, I was just tryin' to explain to him what this picture was doin' to me."

"He probably understands that but like I said, because he loves you, his instincts were ready to take over and I'm puttin' it in a nice way." She said, laughing a little.

"And he'll probably go and talk to Douglas about it but that's okay, it's out now."

"And that's what brothers do, they talk about stuff like this and he's probably glad to have him and James to bounce stuff off of." Marie told her. "So what are you gonna do about this picture?"

"Act like I never saw it amd keep it movin'." She said as she deliberately hit the delete button to erase the haunting image.

You have to because if you keep about all of the stuff that happened to you before the Lord saved you, you never would get anywhere." Marie said with conviction and experience. "We need to concentrate on how we can keep mother up because she really doesn't know what she has yet because today is just her beginning."..

AUGUST 25
TUESDAY

"Man when she laid that one on me there wasn't a thing I could say." Michael remarked with Douglas Tuesday evening. "What do you say to make any kind of difference in a situation like that?"

"Sometimes there are just no words and if she had told me that in the beginning, she might've had it all behind her by now but she didn't."

"She just told you that she was pregnant?"

"She did and we were talkin' about somethin' else altogether and for some reason, she let it out and there I was sort of caught off guard, sittin' right here in this same spot." He said, shaking his head a little.

"And that was how it started with you and her huh?"

"It was and you did the right thing by leavin' the details for Marie to help her with."

"When I saw her pull up I knew it was a God thing because there was that part of me that was ready to calm her down and let her know that there was another way." He said. "And I'm just keepin' it real but I'm findin' out that what happened to me on April nineteenth was a lot more than a good feelin' and all of that good stuff that happens when you first get the Holy Ghost."

"And you know it but I have a question for you." He asked him. "Do you think everything would've been okay if she hadn't showed up when she did?"

"Yeah I do but it did let me know that I can't let my guard down because it could've been different." "But I know that there would've been consequences that wouldn't have been worth it."

"And people are watchin' you, believe it or not."

"I know they are, I'm gettin' stuff everyday at work and it's startin' to be a joke but at this point, it doesn't even matter anymore."

"Then it's a known fact that the baby isn't yours huh?"

"Yeah that's obvious but it's somethin' about it that makes me feel like she is." "Is that crazy or what?"

"You probably feel like that because of your relationship with Janice but you won't really know until she gets here." Douglas said. "And there might be some days when you feel like you don't have to do this or that because she's not yours and that would be a serious mistake." He added with a sobering tone.

"Yeah we've talked about that, and I can tell by the things that she's said how much damage was done because of what she went through."

"It's not a joke and if you had been around when we first found that out, to see firsthand what that did to her, you'd really have a clear understandin' of the responsibility that you're takin' on."

"But I can't get caught up in the biology either, especially after what she just told me." Michael said after a moment. "And when I see the love and concern that you have for her and how you've stepped up and shown her how it's supposed to be, I've got a good idea of what to do or not to do."

"It's somethin' that I had to think and pray about and it was your best friend that planted the seed."

"I didn't know that, how did that happen?"

"I don't know if she had some kind of gut feelin' but she called me one day at work and told me to stop by on my way home." He began.

"And when Mama Frances speaks, you better listen." Michael said.

"Exactly, and what she wanted to do was give me a heads up that Kathryn would be here in a couple of days to take Janice back home to D.C. with her." He continued. "And my first question for her was what that had to do with me, I wasn't gonna come between her and her mother, that was the last thing I was gonna do." "I just happened to be here on the other side of this table when she decided to come out with it and I don't think she had planned on doin' it that way but it is what it is."

"And that's why she felt like you were more involved than you thought huh?"

"She told me that I was one of the main ingredients in the whole mix of things." Douglas said as he recalled the conversation between he and Frances, months before.

"So what was your comeback to that?" "I mean you had to know that you couldn't win man, she's the queen bee." He added as they both laughed.

"I was startin' to get it but I also had to let her know that I wasn't about to try to take her father's place." "Roy was still in the picture and this was before we knew what the truth was but as far as I was concerned, I wasn't goin' there."

"Okay Moses, were you makin' excuses?"

"I wouldn't call it excuses, I was bein' careful about goin' into territory where I didn't belong." "But after she put that on me, it was somethin' I couldn't shake so by the time we found out about William and Kathryn's thing, it was like I didn't have a choice." "If this is what the Lord has for me to do, who am I to ask questions?"

"So it's not like a burden for you to just be there huh?"

"Absolutely not." "And when I find out things like I just did, it makes me realize how much I have to be in a place to make some kind of difference."

"Marie called me last night and Janice said it would be okay if you knew about it but she's not plannin' on lettin' it be a big issue because it can't be changed." Michael said then.

"Then if she doesn't bring it up, I don't have any reason to but this is somethin' that you might have to deal with later on, you know what I'm sayin'?"

"Yeah I've heard about triggers but Sunday was the first time that I had actually seen it happen." "She looked at the picture that his mother sent her of him in his casket and it was almost an instant thing."

"Is that when she told you what happened?" Douglas asked him as he became increasingly concerned.

"She showed me the picture on her phone then she said that it just brought everything back and I thought she meant that it was a reminder of what used to be, you know?" He replied. "Then she went on to say that she hadn't told anybody that he raped her because nobody would believe her."

"So you were the first to know?"

"I was and that was when Marie showed up and that was when I told Janice that I had to leave for a minute, it was just a little too much, I had to go take a walk." He said. "Marie told me that she went into the details with her because she needed to talk about it but I don't need to go there."

"You're right, you don't, but what you can do is be as patient as you can with her because evidently it was a pretty traumatic thing, even though she knew him." Douglas told him. "And sometimes it could be the least little thing that might set her off but the great thing about it is, she has the power of God to help her overcome all of it." He added. "I still remember how I learned how to elevate my mind when that horrible night tried to come back and take me through some changes."

"The motorcycle accident?" Michael asked him.

"It was the worse thing I'd ever seen in my life but I found out about the power I actually had when I did what the scripture told me to do." "I went to a bible class one night and found out about Phillipians four seven and eight and when I learned how to actually do what those verses said, nothin' could bring me down."

"Aunt Frances told me one time that once I found out how to use faith to quench the feiry darts of the wicked, that I already won the fight."

"And you do that by puttin' your faith in what the Word of God says, even when it doesn't seem to make any sense." "That picture that his mother sent her was a device from the enemy to bring her down but when you know where it's comin' from, your battle is already won."

"I guess that's why Marie told me that she'll deal with her from now on." "She's already changed her number so there's no chance that she'll be gettin' anymore stuff from her but if it hadn't been for what she did, we might not have ever known what happened."

"That's one way to look at it and it might be a good thing for you to let her know that she doesn't need to feel guilty about it." "The whole thing is in her past and it's time to move on."...

AUGUST 28
FRIDAY

"Jane has been teaching me about her style of cooking and I just wanted to see if I could do it on my own." Florence remarked Friday afternoon as Marie and Kathryn sat down for lunch at her house.

"So have you been writin' recipes down or just doin' things from memory?" Marie asked her as she dipped into a large bowl of chili with a ladle after blessing the food.

"A little bit of both so I'm hoping that it'll be okay." She said as she sat down across from Kathryn. "And Miss Kathryn you look like you're actually glowing."

"It still feels a little like a dream I had Sunday night and I know that you remember exactly what I mean don't you?"

"It's been a whole month now and I can't put into words how different my life feels." She said. "And when I try to explain things to the people I used to be friends with, they seem to think I've lost my mind or something." She added.

"So you don't feel like they're your friends anymore huh?" Marie asked her.

"They are more like my acquaintances now because they want to be critical about the changes that are going on in my life."

"And that's a good sign that you're doin' what you're should be." Marie said. "I was talkin' to my pastor in D.C. a couple of months ago and he told me somethin' that's really been helpin' me to understand a lot of things." She added as she poured iced tea in her glass.

"Do you mind sharing what he talked with you about?"

"Not at all because what I found out is gonna stay with me for a long time and it might help somebody else." She said. "And it's not anything new or deep but he was explainin' to me how relationships change when you have a new mindset about things after you receive the Holy Ghost." "Then when you try to make it work with people that you used to be close to, it just doesn't work because of the two spirits that are workin' against each other."

"You know, that's really interesting because I've noticed that they're calling less and less and when I do get a chance to talk with them, it's very strained and a little awkward."

"But if they were actin' and sayin' the same things to you, then that might be a problem because they wouldn't be noticin' the change in you." Marie said. "And when I was in the pastor's office that day, he showed me this little bottle of oil and water that he keeps on his desk and he told me to shake it up and tell him what happens."

"Oil and water don't mix." Kathryn remarked.

" That's what he wanted me to see and I've heard that sayin' before but when I actually shook it up and watched it separate after about a minute, I really started to get it." Marie said. "And like she just said, everybody knows that water and oil don't mix, we learned that in science class." "But he had me do it two or three times to help me to see that it doesn't matter how hard you try to make it work, it's not goin' to if you're really serious about livin' right."

"I really do love that illustration, what else did you learn about that?" Florence asked her as she became increasingly intrigued.

"The reason I went to talk to him in the first place was because I was startin' to feel like I was doin' somethin' wrong." She began. "When I went back to work that first week with the Holy Ghost, I didn't feel comfortable doin' the same stuff with the people that I work with and that's when I started to find out how real it is." "And I felt a little bad about tellin' the same people that I used to do things with, that I wasn't goin' there anymore."

"Do you mind sharing a little because I'm experiencing that same thing ."

"Not at all because I know now that if I was still doin' some of the same things I was involved in before, then that would've been a problem." Marie said. "I was goin' to lunch with a couple of people in my department every day and we would sit up and gossip about everybody and talk about our sex lives and all of that kind of stuff that I thought nothin' about, you know what I mean?"

"I think I do." Florence said in agreement.

"And things like that don't seem like that big of a deal if you listen to your own mind instead of what your Holy Ghost is tellin' you not to do and I found that out the hard way."

"Oh my, what happened?"

"Some stuff got back to the person that we were talkin' about one day and she found out some things that were said about her." Marie explained in retrospect. "And I hadn't actually said anything but I was there with the people that were doin' all of the talkin' but I felt like I owed her an apology anyway."

"So was that when you started losing those people as your friends?"

"It was because when they would ask me go out with 'em, I had to start sayin' no because I knew that it would be the same stuff goin' on." "And that's when I started to see that separation happen but I felt so much better because I was startin' to feel condemned." She said, shaking her head. "And I had had enough of that before, and then when he showed me the scripture that said to come out from among them and be separate, I knew it was a done deal."

"Do you remember where that scripture is because I would love to read up on that." Florence said then.

"I think it's in second Corinthians but I'll find it and show it to you before we leave but that really did help me to see what I have to do." She said. "They didn't like it but I can't go back."

"You're right about that, they don't like the fact that I'm going to a church that's really well integrated." Florence began. "They think that's a wrong thing to do and I remember when I thought that way also so I can't judge anyone else but it's caused a separation."

"So how did they find all of this out?"

"It all began when I started talking about how I had seen a miracle in my life and of course I had to explain how it all happened." She recalled. "I told them that Jane's in-laws prayed for me after they found out about the problem I had and that led to a whole new conversation." She said, pausing. "They didn't understand why I let that happen instead of allowing my doctors to begin their treatments, and of course after my second set of X-rays came back, there wasn't much that could be said."

"But you would think that would be good news to anybody that cared anything about you." Kathryn remarked.

"You're absolutely right about that but God was starting to open my eyes about the people that I considered to be close friends." She said. "A lot of them knew how well Jane's father left me when he passed away and of course, that will bring out the best or worst in people."

"In other words, they were your friends because of what they could get out of you." Marie said then.

"That's so true and when they found out that I wouldn't be attending the same church with them anymore, it became even more obvious that the Lord was bringing about a really big change in my life."

"And they had a problem with that huh?"

"They did in the very beginning and it's still going on." She said. "I got a phone call just yesterday from one of the ladies in the book club that we would have every other week." "And she wanted to know when I was going to come to my senses after I told her that I was dropping out because it was interfering with the same time as our bible study." "That comes first now and they don't understand my thinking anymore."

"But you can't expect 'em to and we have to remember how we thought about things before the Lord gave us the Holy Ghost." Marie said. "I have to catch myself sometimes because I might get a little irritated with things that people say and do but when I think about how much love and patience that I saw around here when it was me that needed help, I have to stop and remember where God brought me from."

"That's a wonderful way to look at things and what you just said reminds me of the day that Jane and I went to show Douglas my x-rays after everything came back clean." She said, thinking back. "And I will have to admit, I felt very intimidated by the way he appeared to be." "I'm sitting down across from this handsome guy behind all of this masculine big beard and feeling very afraid." She said, laughing with them.

"We understand." Marie said after a moment.

"I think he must've sensed my fear because he just came out and told me that he was harmless." "And when I look back on it now, I was simply guilty of some very awful racial profiling, but little by little God was beginning to chip all of that away and it actually started on the Sunday afternoon when he and Miss Frances prayed the prayers that healed my condition."

"Was that the day you met him?"

"The very first but the day that he took a look at those x-rays, he actually shed tears and it was then that I knew how caring and loving he was." She anwered. "And that was when we had a serious conversation about my really sad and terrible issues that helped me to see how wrong I had been for years."

"Yeah he has a way of breakin' things down without makin' you feel like the scum of the earth." Marie remarked then. "And he's not judgemental because he knows where he came from."

"You're exactly right and it was because of the way he helped me to look inside of myself that I was able to see how much help

I was in need of." She said. "He explained to me about how I had seen a real miracle which helped me to see that the Lord was giving me another chance to correct my thinking while I had the chance." She continued. "And somehow, the conversation kept going back to our differences and the more we talked about it, the worse I began to feel about myself."

"And you have to get to that place before God can help us because if we're stuck in some kind of self-righteous mode, how do we get our help, you know what I mean?"

"And that's exactly where I was until he started to ask me some very difficult questions that literally showed me how wrong I had been for so long."

"What kind of questions did he ask you and if you don't wanna answer that, I totally understand but since we're here to help each other, it might do us all some good."

"No I don't mind at all and the one thing that he asked me was if I had known that James was married to Christine when I gave him money for his family." She began. "And sadly I had to tell him that I wouldn't have." She continued with obvious regret.

"So what did he have to say about that?" Marie asked her, fascinated.

"I distinctly remember him asking me how I felt about that attitude and that's when I admitted how awful it made me feel." "But what that did was expose myself to myself and as much as it hurt at the time, it was good for me in the long run."

"It made you think huh?"

"I can't put into words how much it made me think and it was like looking into a mirror on the wall and I saw myself turned inside out and it was a very ugly picture looking back at me." She said. "And I don't understand how he knew exactly what to say to me that stirred me up in such a major way."

"You know that has to be a God thing workin' through him because nobody is a mind reader but when you stay close enough to the Lord, he'll use you like that."

"It was actually a little frightening but I started to feel a little better when Irene came out to talk with me because she helped me to see that she used to be in the same dark place."

"I remember her tellin' me the problem she had with Paul when him and Jane got married so it can be on both sides." Marie said. "But you would never know it now because the power of God is so much stronger than all of the stuff that the devil is behind."

"And I was shocked when she told me about her feelings about Jane because I didn't realize that it existed among black people." She admitted. "That's how insulated I was in my safe white world bubble and I actually had no idea that they had a reason to hate that world."

"But can you see now why some black people can be just as off as you were so we really don't have that much room to be talkin' about somebody else." Marie said then after a moment. But we just need to know that it's nothin' but the Holy Ghost that's helpin' us with all of it and your experience is really unusual but it's gettin' the job done."

"Have you asked any of 'em to come to church with you?" Kathryn asked her.

"I haven't done that yet because that's something I'm working up to but when that time comes, I want them to be prepared for an really different worship experience." She concluded. "But that's enough about me, I didn't invite you over to talk about me and I just like being around people that are teaching me how to really love like I'm supposed to."

"It's like a different world and it's made me wonder how I actually survived before this." Kathryn quietly commented.

"That's what we were doin, we were just surviving and sometimes, just barely doin' that but God knows how to order things to happen that sets stuff in motion." Marie remarked as she poured dressing on her salad. "And I said this to Janice a couple of days ago about how her packin' up and movin' here changed so many things for the better for so many of us."

"And I felt bad about that but if she hadn't come here, I wouldn't have known just how much God cares about what we go through, even though we don't deserve that kind of love." Kathryn remarked as she began to "tear up" at the thought of the richness of God's mercy and grace.

"And isn't it amazing when you think about what your life was like this time a year ago and how different it is now?" Florence asked as the tears became contagious.

"I don't even like to think about it but at the same time, you can't forget about how far He's brought you." Marie said. "If you do, it's like takin' all of this for granted and I can't do that." "And I won't try to speak for anybody else, but I couldn't be paid to go back there." She added as she joined the two of them as they all recalled their former circumstances and how they were all delivered in different ways.

"I wonder what somebody would think if they walked in here and saw all three of us sitting here crying like babies." Florence remarked a moment later as she reached for a napkin from the holder.

"It really wouldn't matter because this is such a personal thing between us and the Lord." Marie said, shaking her head a little.

"And we're still goin' through things and I think it would be a good idea if we all just sit here and start to pray for each other." Kathryn suggested. "And I know that had to come from the Lord because I usually don't think that way."

"Get used to that mama, this is just your beginning and you're gonna find out what you've been missin' out on all of this time." Marie told her. "And what we need to do is just put it all out there and not pretend that we're not goin' through." She added."And if it helps, I'll be the first to admit that I'm worried about things that might not even happen."

"Is Jerry still comin' next week?" Kathryn asked her, sensing her apprehension.

"I talked to him a couple of nights ago and he said that was the plan but we'll just see."…

AUGUST 30
SUNDAY

"I might've said this before but I'm tryin' to put myself in her place and in a way, I want her to be here but there's another side that's tellin' me no way." Janice remarked Sunday afternoon as she and Michael sat in the family room with Douglas.

"Marie is takin' care of her because she doesn't want anymore stuff comin' through like what she did last week." Michael told him.

"And that was a good move on her part because that kind of thing is the last thing you need right now." Douglas said. "And you might be surprised at the lengths the devil will go to tryin' to bring you down but the fight is fixed."

"Do you think we're goin' from the fryin' pan into the fire as Aunt Frances says all the time?" Michael asked him, laughing a little.

"You might be, no kiddin', so don't think it strange." He told him. "You just came out of one thing but that experience with Kathryn might have been just gettin' you ready for part two." "And just because she's miles away doesn't make any difference when the Lord is involved and I'm startin' to think that way."

"I know that she could find her way here if she really wanted to get involved but I'm not gonna talk that up." Michael remarked.

"She can be here all she wants but I just don't want her startin' some crazy stuff." Janice commented as they noticed her start to fall apart at the very thought.

"Honey don't over think things, you'll make yourself miserable when you don't have to be." Douglas told her. "But if and when somethin' comes up, you have what it takes to overcome any and all of it." He added as they heard the doorbell.

"Hi, did I come to the wrong house?" Mary Ann Davis asked James after he came to the door.

"Maybe not, who're you lookin' for?"

"Does Janice live here?" She cautiously asked him.

"Yes ma'am she does, did you wanna come in?" He asked her as he opened the door.

"I didn't fly here from Washington D.C. to play games." She said as she slowly came in the entry way.

"Does she know who you are?" James asked her as he picked up on her somewhat callous demeanor, causing a protective instinct to surface.

"We've never seen each other and that's why I'm here." "She's carryin' my dead son's baby and I think I have the right to know who she is." She said, becoming more and more combative. She added as she began to look around. "And why is she livin' like this with white people?"

"I think maybe you need to wait outside for a minute." James told her then as he opened the door back up for her to exit.

"You've got five minutes and if I have to, I know how to get back in here."

"This one is yours, I need for you to do what you do sir." James said a minute later after motioning Douglas out to the hallway. "That's Craig's mother out there and she's got fire in her eyes so go for it."

"Can we help you?" He asked her after coming outside half a minute later.

"Maybe you can and maybe you can't." She said as her defenses began to gradually escalate.

"You're Mary Ann, am I right?" Douglas persisted as he motioned for her to follow him. "Do you feel like takin' a walk?"

"I don't walk with strangers and what do you have to do with Janice?" "That's who I'm here to see."

"We know that but you're goin' through me first." "You can't bogard your way into somebody 's house makin' demands and expect things to go your way ma'am." He told her with gentle but firm authority. "And I'm Janice's adopted father just in case you need to know for some reason." He added before motioning her to follow him again.

"I don't think I got your name, you know mine so we have to be real about this." Mary Ann remarked as she reluctantly followed his lead.

"I'm Douglas Johnson and I met Janice back in February after she left D.C.." He began. "After she found out she was pregnant, she told Craig and he basically told her that that was her problem but that's not what's important now." "She's moved on so when she found out what happened to him, it was a shock but she's not gonna let that get in her way."

"So what is all of this, some kind of group home or somethin'?" She asked, looking back at the house behind them.

"This is her sister and her husband's house that they built last spring and this is where she's gonna be bringin' the baby home."

"So she's livin' with the white guy and her sister in this place that looks like somethin' that a drug dealer built." She said with an air of sarcasm.

"And do you know what?" Douglas said as he suddenly stopped walking. "This is where you get the chip off your shoulder because I'm not allowin' you to go in there with this foul spirit that you have." He quietly told her with bold authority.

"Then you tell me how I'm supposed to feel since you seem to know so much about me." She immediately came back as slow tears began to come down her face.

" We need to sit down and talk about it like we have some sense." He said as he directed her back up on the small porch where they could sit down.

"Do you have children?" She asked him a few moments later, coming right to her point as they sat down.

"I do, I have six." He began. "And I realize that Craig was the only one you had and we understand why you want to be in his baby's life but there's a way to do it."

"What do you mean there's a way to do it?" "I went through a lot of trouble to find out where she is and I'm not goin' back until I see and talk to her." She told him with pleading in her voice.

"And there's no doubt about that but we need to get an understanding first." "Even though she's eighteen years old, I'm serious about what God gave me to do."

"Why do you have to put God in this?"

"That's a whole separate issue and I'm not goin' there because I don't think that's what you want to hear right now." "I know that you're still hurt about what happened to Craig, and maybe when you talk to Janice, she might be able to say or do somethin' to help you but like I said before, there's a way to do it." He told her. "You can't just barge into somebody's house and demand to have your way because that doesn't do anything but turn everybody off and make people resist you."

"I apologize for that but that doesn't change anything, I still need to see her."

"I understand that so here's what I'm gonna do." He said pausing as he reached for his phone from his shirt pocket. "I'll text her and have her come out here then I'll get out of the way so you two can have a conversation."

"I can't believe this." Janice said a minute later as she showed the text to Michael that informed her that Mary Ann was waiting outside.

"C'mon, you can do this." He told her as he helped her stand up.

"How did she find out where I am?"

"We can find that out later but right now, just be as nice as you can be and get it over with." He told her. "We got your back whatever happens."

"How in the world did you end up here with the white folks and the corn fields?" Mary Ann asked as she and Janice sat in the livingroom a few minutes later behind closed French doors.

"I decided to come here because I needed somewhere to go when my parents told me to find somewhere else to live when I told 'em that I was pregnant." Janice said after a moment. "And I know that probably sounds crazy or old fashioned and all of that but that's what happened."

"And this is your sister's house I was told." Mary Ann said, still determined to "get to the bottom" of things.

She nodded. "We just moved out here in May and you don't have to worry about anything when it comes down to Kristen havin' what she needs because I'm workin' and it's all gonna be okay."

"When did you tell Craig?"

"As soon as I found out." Janice said as she recalled the day. "I sent him a text and he said that it was my problem, not his." She added as she felt herself start to crumble as she remembered his response."And you might not believe me when I tell you this but he raped me in the men's restroom at work one night just because I asked him for a ride home." She added with an air of anger mixed with stress as she began to recall the traumatic details of the experience.

"My son wouldn't have done that, he wasn't that way." Mary Ann responded.

"Then maybe you didn't know him like you thought you did." Janice came back as she began to feel the strength of her spirit rise to the occasion. "And I came really close to gettin' an abortion but I didn't have anymore money after I bought the plane ticket to get here."

"So that's the only reason that you didn't?"

She shook her head. "After I got here and they found out what was goin' on with me, Douglas was the first one to tell me that wasn't an option."

"Douglas is that guy that I was just talkin' to out there?" She asked her.

Janice nodded before speaking again. "He was the first one I told after I moved here." She began. "I was afraid to tell anybody because I thought the same thing would happen all over again but I knew I wasn't gonna be able to keep it too long." She continued as she vividly remembered the conversation. "He just happened to be the one that was takin' time to listen to my problems and out it came."

"Is he some kin to you or somethin'?"

"He's my sister's husband but after a lot of other things happened, he just stepped in and has done what nobody else would." She replied. "The man that I grew up with turned out not to be my real father and that whole thing hurt me more than anything in my life and he was there to fill in the gaps."

"So that tells me that you and Craig were just friends." Mary Ann surmised.

"He was just my co-worker and after what he did to me, I almost hated him so when he told me that this baby wasn't his problem, I wasn't hurt because I didn't love him." Janice admitted to her. "But all of that is in my past, I've moved on because I found out how to start all over again and the Lord is helpin' me to not hold that against him, even though he's gone." Janice said as she took the opportunity to "testify."

"And how old are you?"

"I turned eighteen right before I moved here in February and a lot of people have told me that I sound older than that but I have to grow up, I'm gonna have a baby to take care of in about a month."

"Do you think you'll know what to do if she gets sick and have you thought about day care and all of that when you go back to work?" Mary Ann threw at her.

"How come you're bein' so hostile, I have all of that under control." Janice replied as she felt herself tense up in reaction to a mild contraction.

"You might think you do and when you're tryin' to do all of that by yourself, it's even harder than it would be if you had somebody helpin' you." She said. "I've been there, I had to raise Craig with no support from anybody because his father was married to somebody else and he didn't want any part of it."

"Can you tell me why you sent that dead picture of him?" Janice asked her, completely ignoring the fiery dart intended to discourage her as she felt strength rise up within her.

"I sent it to you because I felt that my grandbaby needed to have some idea of what he looked like." She answered after a moment.

"In a casket??" Janice asked her. "There's no way and I deleted it so she won't ever see it but if you have a picture that I can show her when she's old enough to understand some stuff, then that's a little different." She added as Frances tapped on the door and walked slowly in.

"Everything okay in here?" She asked as she sat down in a nearby chair. "I just found out that you were here and anytime somebody comes in the place where I live, I think I need to have a converation with'em." She said cordially.

"I'm here from D.C. and I just wanted to meet this girl that's havin' my only grandchild and I don't see anything wrong with that." Mary Ann answered her. "Is this your house?" She asked as she looked around.

"This is my daughter and her husband's house but I live here and I know about everything that goes on in this place." She said. "And when I hear the spirit of the Lord tell me to do somethin', I have to do it and that's why I came in here." "Would you like some dinner, there's a lot of food back there and you're welcomed to anything you see." She offered. "And I'm Frances, I apologize for not tellin' you what my name is and I'm who Janice calls Aunt Frances."

"Just one big happy family huh?" Mary Ann asked with sarcasm in her voice.

"If that's the way you'd like to put it sweetheart, that's fine, but you can't come in here stirrin' up trouble because of what's been goin' on in your life." "We can help you and take time with you but we're not intimidated by the things you're bringin' in here." Frances told her. "We love your grandchild just as much as you do and we're not tryin' to keep her away from you but she'll be well taken care of if that's what you're worried about."

"She's eighteen years old and it's gonna be hard as you know what to bring her up and all I'm askin' is that you let me help you." She said, turning to Janice.

"I don't have a problem with that but I feel like you're gonna try to just take over and that won't work." Janice told her.

"But don't you think I have a right to make some decisions about the things that go on in her life?" "I don't have anybody else and I want to be involved, is that so wrong?" She added as her voice elevated in frustration.

"I'm not doin' this right now because I don't wanna end up sayin' somethin' that I shouldn't." Janice said then as she slowly got up from the sofa.

"Go on back in there with Michael and Douglas, we'll be in there later." Frances told her then.

"Who in the world is Michael?" "I know who that other guy was but who is Michael?" She demanded.

"Honey you need to calm yourself down because everything is under control." Frances told her without hesitation. "And I'm gonna be up front with you because that's what I feel led to do." She added after a short moment.

"I didn't come all this way to be treated like I don't have any sense lady." Mary Ann told her. "Who is Michael?" She insisted.

"Michael is probably gonna be the one to raise your grandbaby and we don't have a problem with you wantin' to know who he is." Frances told her. "You have the right to know but if you give him a chance, I think you'll like what you see from him."

"How in the world did that happen?" "What did she do, decide to find somebody that's gonna take care of her baby because she can't do it by herself?" "I don't know what kind of set up all of this is but men don't do that." "Is he here?"

"Calm yourself down and I'll make sure you see him and get a chance to talk to him, but not until you get this chip off your shoulder and let us help you with this." Frances told her. "Do you feel like dinner?" She offered again.

She didn't answer but sat there attempting to process the whole scenario that she had just experienced, totally different from what she had anticipated.

"When was the last time somebody showed you a little love?" Frances asked as she got up and came towards her before sitting down and embracing her as she yielded to the leading of the Holy Ghost.

"There's nobody around, my son was all that I had and now he's gone." She managed to say through her lingering pain as she began to "open up" as never before. "He was the only thing that I was livin' for and all I want to do is to be in his baby's life."

"You will be and God knows what you're feelin' right now and I think that's why somehow you ended up here." "We don't know how you got here but He has a way of doing things that we don't always understand."

"But why did God take the only thing that I had in this world?" Mary Ann asked her. "And do you know how much trouble I went through to find out where Janice is?"

"We don't have to know and it's up to you if you want to let us know but the important thing is that you're in a place where we can help you." Frances told her. "The Lord is the head of this house and we want you to feel some peace in here because you've been through a lot of stress with this."

She nodded a little then before speaking. "And I really didn't mean to run her off like that but I started to panic when I heard you talk about another man that's gonna be in the baby's life." "That's scary to me because I don't want her to grow up like I did."

"I understand that but you're thinkin' too far ahead of things, you're better off takin' one day at a time." Frances patiently told her. "We're gonna help you get through today and I think it'll be good for you to sit down and talk to Michael, he's here but I'll leave that up to you."

"I moved here from St. Louis when I lost my job down there." Michael remarked ten minutes later after sitting down with Mary Ann. "And I'm gonna be really upfront about this because I think I know where you're goin' but I'm used to people critcizin' me and it doesn't matter anymore." He added.

"But don't you think I have a right to know who's gonna be in this baby's life?"

"You do and I don't have a problem with that but jumpin' to conclusions when you don't know that much about what's goin' on isn't quite the way to handle this." He told her, remaining patient but "standing up" to her attempt to rattle him.

"Are you some kin to that guy that I was talkin' to outside?" She asked him then as she "studied" him.

"Yes ma'am, we're brothers." "Can you tell?"

"Yeah I can." "Did he introduce Janice to you so she could have somebody to help take care of the baby?"

"No that's not what happened but that's not really important." "And I'm not gonna pretend that I can prove anything to you when it comes to this baby that's not even here yet."

"I just need for you to know that if there's a problem with any kind of neglect or abuse of her, you're in big trouble with me." She told him. "I worked for C.P.S. for five years and I know how the system works." She said.

"Like I just said, I don't have to prove anything to anybody except Janice and things like that don't scare me." Michael responded. "This whole thing is somethin' that we've prayed about so there's not much that you can do except be thankful that she won't grow up without a father."

"My son was her father so you can't go there with me young man."

"I have to go there because he was the one that told Janice that this was her problem and not his." Michael came back. "And we're not gonna try to keep her away from you, that wouldn't be fair but since Craig isn't here, I'm the one that she'll know as her father." "We all know that it's not blood and all of that but that doesn't always mean anything." He emphasized with a spirit of boldness.

"You just need to keep in mind that I have connections and it doesn't matter that I'll be across country because you see I was able to find Janice." She said after a moment. "I know that she changed her number and all of that crap but when I sent her Craig's funeral picture, I found out where this place was so I can thank technology for that." She said with toxic sarcasm.

"Maybe so but I think I need to let you know that we don't fight our own battles so if somethin' crazy goes down, it won't go anywhere." Michael told her with confidence and trust in God.

"Let's go get you a plate, you look like you can use a good meal." Frances told her then as she got up from her chair then. "I think that both of you have had enough for right now so it's time to move on to somethin' else."

"I feel kind of bad for walkin' out like I did but she was sayin' things that were makin' me wanna say stuff that I would have to apologize for later." Janice remarked, back in the family room with Douglas. "I was startin' to have contractions in there because she was makin' me tense up." She added, laughing a little at herself.

"That'll be happenin' more and more the closer you get but you did the right thing by just walkin' away from it because you don't wanna take her to another level in here."

"I mean she was talkin' to me like I had done somethin' off, I'm just tryin' to get myself together because I know everything is about to change."

"And she knows that you haven't done anything, but she probably needs somebody to take her feelings out on and you're the one that's closest to the whole situation." Douglas told her. "You're the only one that's connected to what's left of him and she might be goin' about it the wrong way but you have to be able to overlook that spirit that's drivin' her to act like she is."

"Like how?" She asked in frustration mixed with the desire to come to a peaceful solution to the new "problem" in her life.

"I know it'll probably rub you the wrong way but you're gonna have to get out of your comfort zone and do exactly the opposite of what your mind wants to do or say." He answered . "Janice wants to go in there and tell her to go back where she came from but that's not what the Lord is expectin' out of you or any of the rest of us that say we have the Holy Ghost."

She nodded in agreement then.

"And I'm not sayin' that because it might sound like the right thing but I lived through things with Irene from the night that I came home with another spirit than I woke up with that day." He continued. "I made the mistake of thinkin' that she would be glad about it but I got a revelation real quick that I had a fight on my hands." "She would do things on purpose just to see what my reaction would be and it wasn't an easy thing to give in and take down with her but I was determined that Junkyard was not comin' back."

"And it paid off huh?"

"It did and the Lord is not gonna lead you wrong with this so just calm down a little and let God help you."

"Are you okay?" Janice asked Mary Ann a few minutes later after coming back over to the livingroom where she found her sitting alone on the sofa.

"I told both of them to leave me alone for a few minutes so that's why I'm in here by myself." Mary Ann answered her after a moment.

"I'm sorry that I got up and left but I felt like you were tryin' to take everything over and I just didn't wanna get into any kind of argument." Janice explained as she slowly sat back down.

"I met your friend Michael." She said with obvious resentment.

"Do you have a problem with him?"

"Did he know that you were pregnant when he met you?" She asked, ignoring her question.

She nodded.

"Then why would he get involved with somebody that's havin' somebody else's baby?" "That doesn't make sense to me and I'm gonna be nervous about him because this kind of thing never works." "This whole set up is bizarre and I'm really uncomfortable with it."

"So what do you want us to do?" "We can't prove anything to you so what do you want us to do?" Janice asked her again as she kept her composure.

"Is he gonna marry you or what?"

"We're still talkin' about that but he's tryin' to wait until after she's born before we get engaged." She told her.

"And that's the problem with men, they like to talk but when it comes down to action, they come up with a bunch of excuses about why they won't keep their word."

"Did you wanna see the nursery upstairs?" Janice asked her, refusing to get caught up in a useless conversation.

"You already have a nursery done?" "When is your due date?"

"September twenty-third but my doctor said since this is my first baby, she might come a week later." Janice said in an attempt to include her in the "details."

"How did you do this?" Mary Ann asked her five minutes later after following her to the prepared nursery upstairs, down at the end of the hallway.

"A lot of people have given me things and I started savin' money right after I started workin'." Janice said as she sat down on the edge of her bed.

"How much do you have to pay him to live here?" Mary Ann asked, looking around the room. "I mean I don't mean to get into your business but this just seems too good to be true for you."

"We agreed on a hundred a month but that's because I do a lot of baby sittin' and other stuff around here so it all worked out."

"So your sister is married to that white guy that came to the door when I got here." Mary Ann concluded then, trying to put all of the facts together.

She nodded. "When they found out I was pregnant, he got me a job where he works and that's how I'm takin' care of stuff." "I bought a car and I have a payment but I don't want you to worry about Kristen because God is gonna take care of us."

"Just that simple huh?"

"So much has happened to me since I moved here that it has to be God that has been in all of my details, and it would be wrong if I gave myself any credit for any of this." Janice said as she recognized the opportunity to "make her boast" in the Lord. "And if I had stayed in D.C., I'd probably be in a really bad place right now."

"But that's where you were born and grew up wasn't it?" Mary Ann asked. "I love D.C. and I just don't understand why you'd come here of all places."

"When my parents found out about me, they told me to find someplace else to live and I know that probably sounds out of date or whatever but that's what they told me." Janice responded. "And I've got cousins here so I didn't know what else to do." "I had some money saved up and I bought a one way plane ticket here and just showed up one Sunday night." She said as she recalled the circumstances. "Nobody knew about it because I was scared to say anything but I knew I had to either tell somebody or get an abortion and that's when Douglas told me that wasn't an option so here I am."

"And I hope you're not sorry about that are you?"

"I'm not and all I needed was for somebody to tell me not to and he was the one that let me know he cared enough about what I was goin' through."

"So that's why you call him your adopted father huh?"

She nodded. "The man that I thought was my father for eighteen years died and so did my biological father but God took care of that too." Janice told her as she felt more help swell up in her as she continued to give God the glory.

"Does your mother know about all of this?" She asked as she continued to "take it all in".

"She knows about everything that's happened and she moved here a couple of months ago."

"Then she'll be here when you have the baby and I'll be back in D.C. missin' out on it." She said with obvious resentment.

"About all I can do is send you pictures of her, I can't really do anything else right now.

"What if I paid you to come and stay there for awhile?" She asked.

"Are you serious?" Janice asked in amazement. "I might bring her to see you when she gets old enough to travel but I don't want anything to do with that place." "I've got too many bad memories and the Lord delivered me from that environment that I was in and gave me a whole new start when I moved here." She added as tears began to flow at the thought of how far she had come.

"You'd better be strong girl, you have a baby on the way." Mary Ann said as she totally misunderstood what seemed like a weak moment in her.

Janice shook her head then before speaking. "You don't understand, I'm like this because I'm so thankful for the way God brought me up and out of where I was this time last year." "I didn't know what it felt like for somebody to love me and I know now how to think about somebody else beside myself and all of that means a lot to me." She said in her own defense. "And I can't let anybody take me backwards and that's what I would be doin' if I went back there, I can't do it." She said as Marie appeared in the doorway then.

"Hey, I found you." She remarked. "Everything okay?" She asked Janice.

She nodded.

"I'm Marie, Janice's sister." She told her after a moment.

"You don't look anything alike." She said as if she didn't believe her.

"We have different fathers, maybe that's why." Marie said in a matter of fact tone as she sat down next to Janice on her bed. "So how did you find us?" She asked her, getting right to the point.

"If you have a cell phone number, you can trace anybody honey, it wasn't hard." "And I was talkin' to your sister-

"And you're out of order by comin' in here stirrin' up trouble when everything's under control." Marie said as she gently but forcibly used her God given authority to overcome this power of darkness that was intending to disrupt the peace of God that passes all understanding. "We know that you're here because you want to be involved as this baby's grandmother and we understand that but all of this hostility just doesn't have a place in here."

"Do you live here too?" She asked with the same air of contention that she displayed since her arrival, unmoved by anything she had said.

For right now I do but I'm here from D.C. to help our mother while she's in rehab for a couple of months."

"So she doesn't live there anymore?" Mary Ann threw at her. "Why should she have the chance to be here while I'm missin' out on everything?"

"Do you any vacation time on your job that you can use?" Marie asked her.

"I had to use the time that I had to get my son buried and the whole thing is so unfair to me!" She said, raising her voice in anger. "I didn't do anything to deserve what I got and all of this talk about God this and God that, is rubbin' me the wrong way because where was God the night my son lost his life?" She challenged them with raging bitterness. "He was the only thing I had and now he's out of the picture so all I want to do is to be around for his daughter but I don't see that happenin' because of all of this." She said waving one of her arms around the room with obvious resentment.

"All of what, we're not tryin' to keep you away from her, where did you get that from?" Marie asked her.

"If I had known that this is what I would be walkin' into, I wouldn't have even bothered to come." "This whole place makes me feel like I'm not good enough to be here and I'm not comfortable with my grandchild bein' around these white folks that I've seen in here."

"Are you serious?" Marie asked her.

"I'm very serious, and I'm not just goin' away and act like it's nothin' to worry about." She continued. "It was a white guy that killed Craig and I can't just sit by and watch his baby grow up with people that are probably gonna mistreat her just because she's black."

"You're gettin' too far ahead of things so this is where we end all of the stuff that you're bringin' in here." Marie told her after a moment. "We're gonna do everything we can to make sure that Kristen knows who you are and that's all we can do right now."

"But this is between Janice and me, you really don't have that much to say about it."

"Then I'm through talkin' about it because there's no more to say." Janice spoke up then. "Do you wanna go downstairs and get somethin' to eat?" She asked, repeating France's offer.

"It depends on what it is, and I'm not eatin' nothin' that was thrown together by white people so excuse me if I'm bein' difficult but that's the way it is."

"That's up to you, we're not tryin' to force anything on you." Marie told her in a matter of fact way, refusing to escalate the conversation as she noticed a text from Douglas downstairs, informing her that he was coming up.

"Are you gonna be here long?" Janice asked her in an attempt to calm her antagonism.

"I flew here and got a rental car because I'm goin' to Kansas City for a couple of weeks." She said shortly. "I have a sister that lives down there and I decided to stop here on the way to see what was goin' on with you." She continued. "And you can believe that I'm gonna be stoppin' by on my way back to to D.C. to make sure that you're takin' care of yourself because I don't need anymore trouble in my life, do you get it young lady?"

Instead of answering, their attention switched over to Douglas who appeared in the doorway then.

"So why do you have a gun in here?" He calmly asked Mary Ann a moment later who then looked at him in shock with a loss for words.

"Nobody in here has anything against you but this is the choice you have." He said pausing with quiet but powerful authority. "You either get it out of here and come back in if you're not done talkin' or leave and not bring it back." He added without reservation. "That pistol that you're packin' can't be in this house so the choice is yours."

She said nothing as she began to squirm nervously in the rocker that she was sitting in. Neither spoke as their eyes locked before she slowly stood up and cautiously headed towards the doorway as if in fear of him.

"Sweetheart I'm harmless but I'm serious when it comes to doin' what God leads me to do." He told her as he sensed her hesitation. "You're welcomed to stay as long as you want but you don't need any kind of weapons in here." He added as he started walking behind her to make sure she left the house.

"Do I believe what I just saw?" Janice asked in mild shock a moment later.

"We saw it and this is what we have to do when we come across that kind of spirit in people." Marie said. "I'm gonna talk to him later on and find out what made him come up here but I think both of us already know what's goin' on." She added as Janice began to cry tears of relief and stress that had been brought on by Mary Ann's unnecessary venom.

"Is she leavin'?" Janice asked after Marie got up and went over to the window where she watched Mary Ann get in the rental car and quickly drive off.

"Yeah she's gone but today is probably not the last time you'll hear from her so just take this one day at a time." Marie told her. "And you've got what, four weeks before everything in your life changes?"

She nodded. "Is Michael okay?" She asked, concerned about his reaction after Mary Ann's "attack" on him.

"He's good, don't worry about him." She assured her. "This isn't the first time he's had to deal with somebody else's stuff and he's probably gettin' used to it by now, you know what I mean?"

"I understand why he might get tired of people gettin' into his business and I just hope she backs off after today because it's startin' to get close and I don't need anything extra."

"She might be back so just keep your guard up but I don't think she'll wanna run into Douglas again." Marie said shaking her head. "And I don't think he was tryin' to scare her but he had to do what he had to do and it worked."

"Man it was like she showed up on cue, it was unreal." Michael remarked as he sat down in James' office with him. "We were in there talkin' to Douglas about what might happen with her and then she shows up like out of nowhere."

"When I opened the door she probably thought she was at the wrong house and I could tell right away that she might be a problem." James said. "And that's why I had Douglas come out to deal with her, I wasn't goin' there."

"Did she scare you off man?" Michael asked as they both laughed.

"Scared is not the word but I had other things to do and I could tell that it wouldn't have been good if I had gotten on her bad side."

"Kind of a bad vibe huh?"

"I've had run ins with other people like that and I don't trust me." "There's no good thing in my flesh and after I had to go back and apologize to Miss Florence, I told myself never again." "Just shut up and keep it movin'."

"I was about to get there then I remembered somethin' that Aunt Frances told me one time about the tongue bein' a world of fire and how much trouble it can get you in."

"And you know it and it's even harder when you know you have truth on your side so I guess it's a matter of keepin' yourself humble." James said. "I found that out when my mother turned on Chris out of nowhere and if it hadn't been for the Lord sendin' Douglas my way to help me through that, it would've been a really bad thing."

"Did she ever tell you why she changed up like that?"

"I never did figure that out and sometimes I think she was against it from the start but she was just puttin' on an act just to keep stuff under control." He began. "And even if she had come out with it from the start, that wouldn't have changed my mind because both of us knew what was up." "We knew that we were gonna have problems that most couples don't because of the race thing but we kept prayin' about it and by the time we had been together for a year, we didn't have any doubt about it."

"And that's why I can't let people get next to me because I know what we've been talkin' to the Lord about."

"Are you about ready to put the ring on her finger?"

"I have it and I'm really tryin' to wait til after the baby's born but sometimes I feel like there's no point in waitin', especially when she's havin' days like today, you know what I mean?"

"Yeah there's somethin' about that ring that makes it a little easier to get stuff planned and it might seem a little old school to a lot of people but you can't lose by doin' it the right way."

"We did like a walk through the house a couple of days ago so I can get an idea of how she wants it so if you have the time, I need to get an estimate from you."

"If you can get a list together I can probably come up with a number for you in a couple of days."

"Number one is no more carpet and I went to look at the price of laminate just to get an idea of what it'll take."

"Do you have an idea about how many square feet you're talkin' about?"

"I asked Aunt Frances about that and she doesn't remember exactly but she said there's a file cabinet down in the basement that has all of the house information in an envelope." He said after thinking a moment.

"When you find that out, then decide on what you want and you might be able to find some laminate on clearance somewhere and come out cheaper." He said as Marie walked in.

"Okay if I come in guys?" She asked as she slowly walked in.

"Well why not, my house is your house." James told her.

"Is your friend still here?" Michael asked her as she sat down with her plate.

"You missed the drama up there, Douglas showed up in the nursery where we tryin' to talk to her." She began.

O-Kay, you know you can't stop there don't you?" Michael asked her, anxious to hear about what had transpired.

"Of course not, that's why I had to find you." "I sent Janice over there to Paul and Jane's where mother is hangin' out with Miss Florence."

"Those two are a perfect match, God sure does know how to do things." James remarked. "So what went down ma'am?"

"Janice took her upstairs so she could see Kristen's nursery and then she went off about some other stuff that wasn't makin' much sense." Marie said, recalling the conversations. "She started goin' off about how it was a white guy that killed Craig and she didn't want any food that any white people had cooked and it was really gettin' crazy." She said, pausing. "Then I get this text from Douglas tellin' me that he was on his way up."

"Uh oh." Michael said.

"Yeah tell me about it and I didn't say a word, we just kept listenin' to what she had to say." She said. "And when I think about it, I get the impression that she's been by herself a lot and she's just mad at the world in general and it's a little hard to help people like that."

"You can't help somebody that doesn't know that there's a problem and maybe she doesn't." James said then.

"Maybe not but Douglas came up there and asked her why she had a gun in here." Marie said, waiting on their reaction.

"What??" Michael asked her in total surprise.

"You heard me and she couldn't say a word." "It was like watchin' the I.D. channel in real time, I'm not kiddin." Marie said then. "And I think she was so shocked that she couldn't think of anything to say."

"How did all of this happen and we didn't know about it?" Michael asked.

"This is a big house and things can go on and you'd never know it."

"Chris tells me all of the time that we need a intercom system in here and that'll probably happen eventually." "But finish what you started ma'am, you can't keep us hangin'." He told her.

"He told her that she either had to get her gun out of here or leave and the choice was hers and he was as sweet as he could be but she tell that he was not playin'."

"I can just see it, he probably gave her a look that probably put the fear of God in her." Michael said, shaking his head at the thought.

"She seemed to be afraid to move and that's when he told her that he was harmless but serious as a heart attack with her."

"Where is he now, did you talk to him after she left?" Michael asked her.

"He followed her out to make sure she left the house and I watched her drive out of here like somebody was chasin' her, but I haven't seen him, I don't know where he went."

"Irene told me one time when he does things like that, he has to go off and be by himself for a minute so maybe that's what he's doin'." Michael said. "I could text him, but I'm not goin' there, I'm stayin' out of his space for right now."

"And you know it." "If he wants to talk about it, he will but I'm not gonna bring it up because there's really nothin' to say."

"The action did all of the talkin' huh?"

"You wouldn't believe how smooth it went and that tells me that it had to be the Lord behind what he did."

"But how do you get to that place, he just seems to know what to do and when to do it and it always works."

"I was talkin' to Terry on Thursday night at church and she told me that she can't wait to get home at night so she can lay in her bed and listen to him pray like a crazy man." Marie said, laughing a little.

"His office is down the hall from that room and I'd do the same thing, it was unreal." Michael said as he recalled the same experience.

"It takes a lot of time to get there like that and for both of you it hasn't been six months has it?" James asked them.

They both simultaneously shook their heads in understanding of his question.

"Not even six months yet so I get it but I guess you have to start somewhere." Michael remarked.

"You do but he used to be where you are and it takes time and a lot of experiences with the Lord to get there, believe me." James said, reassuring them. "And he told me not too long ago when we were talkin' about the fight between what your flesh wants and what your spirit is tellin' you to do." He continued. "He said when the Lord was dealin' with him about his prayer life probably about five or six years ago, he said he remembered how easy it had been for him to get high and drunk, so it shouldn't be a problem for him to do what was right for what matters."

"In other words, get it together." Marie said then.

"Pretty much." "And he said when he started to see results, that was what got him to where he is now, and it's like he's as much addicted to crashin' the throne as he was to that other stuff out there that would've probably killed him."

"That's a scary thought." Michael remarked.

"It is and he never has let himself forget how close he came to goin' out and that's why he doesn't let up when it comes to workin' with people."

"And if she comes back, they might end up face to face again and that would be a real interestin' picture to see." Marie said. "But nothin' surprises me anymore."…

Chapter 2

September 2
Wednesday

"She told me that there was a file cabinet down in the basement when she signed the deed over but I didn't think any more about it 'til Sunday." Michael remarked with Douglas down in his office Wednesday evening as he handed him an envelope that he had found. "I was talkin' to James about some stuff that I'm plannin' to do in the house and that was in there behind the original blueprint." He added as he pulled out four certificates of deposits that William had purchased nearly forty years earlier.

"Are you kiddin' me?" Douglas asked after examining the

documents with Paul, Irene, Chris and Donna's names printed on each of them.

"I looked at those and the first thing I thought was how in the world could they still be there after almost forty years?"

"Either your best friend didn't know these were there or she just forgot about 'em." Douglas said, referring to Frances. "So what you need to do is to make sure she knows about these and you can go from there."

"Yeah that's the next thing but are you thinkin' the same thing that I am?"

"First things first but I really don't think it would be a problem to make sure that Janice is included in all of this because he was just as much her father as he was theirs." He said as he continued to look over the C.D.s. "But I wouldn't say anything until all of 'em know about these."

"There's no way but is there a way to figure out how much they're worth now?" He asked then. "And I'm just curious about how those work, don't get the wrong idea man." He said.

"It depends on the interest rate that these have earned over the last thirty years, so the first thing you need to do is make sure she knows about this so she can make a trip to the bank." He emphasized again after a moment.

"I'll call her tomorrow and let her know what's goin' on."Michael said, pausing. "But in the mean time, not to change the subject, I'm just about ready to start makin' things official with Janice and me." He said, waiting on his reaction.

He nodded in agreement. "It's probably about time but before you do that, it would probably do you some good to give yourself a man to man talk like you never have before in your life." Douglas told him with an unmistakable soberness in his voice. "You're about to take on somethin' that most men wouldn't do and you're not just marryin' her, but you're takin' on a responsibility that you didn't have anything to do with, and it's gonna take the help of the Lord to get you through it."

Michael nodded then as he felt himself yield to his emotions at the gravity of the words that he had just heard.

"And I don't mean to try to discourage you because I think you're lettin' God lead you but I believe in bein' up front and honest about stuff like this so it won't take you by surprise one day."

"Give me all you got man because I know it's not what I'm used to doin' and after what happened on Sunday, I'm just about ready for anything." Michael said. "And Marie told us what happened up there and I just wanna know how that went down."

"It was one of those things when your spirit reveals somethin' to you, that you can't waste any time wonderin' about it." He said after a moment. "And it takes time and experience to learn how to tell the difference between your mind and what the Lord is tellin' you."

"But what we were tryin' to figure out was how sure you were about it." Michael said. "When Marie told us what went down with that woman, it sounded pretty bizarre."

"It's not bizarre when you learn how to walk in the spirit that God gave you but you don't get there over night." "You learn by not bein' obedient to what that still small voice tells you and causin' yourself some problems that didn't have to happen but that's all a part of the learnin' process."

"That's why we're bein' so cautious about this marriage thing because we know that once it's done, we're not undoin' it and that's not what we're used to, you know what I mean?"

"I know exactly what you mean and I feel led to remind you that both of you will have the responsibility of teachin' this child that she has a soul and that's the most important part of her existance." He emphasized. "You can make sure she has enough food and clothes and all of that good stuff but the earlier she knows who Jesus is, the better because the way this world is goin', we can't rely on nothin' or nobody else."

"Man you don't know how glad I am that I'm gettin' this kind of talk from you because it's helpin' me to keep it real."

"We have to keep it real but because we have the power of the spirit of God, there's nothin' that can overcome you if you allow it to work." Douglas said. "And back to what happened on Sunday, I had moved on from Miss Mary Ann, I was out on the deck talkin' to Terry and Sheila, workin' with a spare rib." He said as he thought back to the moment. "And it was as clear as you and me sittin' here, "she has a gun."

"Man that is some deep stuff." Michael remarked. "And Marie said that you came up there and told her what was up and she couldn't say a word."

"What could she say?" "And I didn't do that to scare her but she had to know that that couldn't happen in there." He said."And I learned a long time ago that our arms are too short to box with God and she almost had to know what was goin' on."

"So she didn't try to argue with you or say she didn't have it huh?"

"She didn't say word one and it was none of my business that she had one but it just couldn't be in the house." "She might've even had a permit but the way she was talkin' and actin' in there, you can't take chances." "When you're upset and mad at the world in general, you do things on impulse sometimes and I'm sayin' that from experience." He added. "When I was out there, I didn't leave the house without Brutus."

"Brutus?" Michael asked, amused.

"That was the name I gave that forty-five that went everywhere with me." "You're probably too young to remember the Popeye cartoons but Brutus was a bully that intimidated everybody so that's where that came from." He said, laughing with him. "I would walk into a club and the first thing they'd say was Junkyard and Brutus are in the house, watch out."

"So you know what's up with her huh?"

"I really do, you're right." "I've been where she is and I can't be so quick to pass judgement on her because I know if it wasn't for the mercy and grace of God, I'd be gone by now or decomposin' in prison somewhere." He said, shaking his head at the thought. "And I wouldn't be at all surprised when she shows back up so what you need to do is keep her in your prayers because this might be the beginnin' of somethin' that'll be a life changer for you."

"She's gonna make Miss Kathryn look like a walk in the park huh?"

"Could be but the main thing that you have to remember is to keep your integrity, and not let anything she might do or say cause you to be out of the will of God." He told him. "I can remember when Irene would try her best to take me back to where I came from, and if I hadn't been on my guard, she would've taken me there but you have to have a desire to be kept."

"And when I think about the stuff that she was sayin', what it did was teach me how to keep my mouth shut because truth was on my side and I really didn't have anything to worry about."

"And like you said, this woman that we met on Sunday might make Kathryn look like a bed of roses, but God knows us better than we know ourselves." "He knows what needs to be added and what needs to be taken out of us and the sooner we submit and let Him do what He does with us, the better off we'll be." He said with known conviction.

"That's what the Holy Ghost is for huh?"

"You got it and you never know why God allows things to happen like this, but one thing I think that I understand about her is the lack of love in her life." He said after a moment. "She just lost the most important thing in her life and now that she knows that she'll have this baby to hold on to, she's gonna do any and everything to be around her."

"You don't think she would actually move here do you?" Michael asked him with obvious angst.

"Anything is possible but the best thing for you to do is to stay in touch with the Lord about her because that's your best defense." He told him. "And if and when you see her again, I think it would help if you can get past all of that rough exterior and try to see the need of the soul behind all of that because that's what really matters."

"When I was talkin' to her, it was like tryin' to bust down a brick wall because she would shoot down everything I had to say." Michael said then. "And I was tryin' to put myself in her place so I could understand where she was comin' from but I'm startin' to find out how cheap talk is." "I'm done tryin' to convince people to see what this is all about with Janice and me and this baby that everybody seems to have such a problem with." He added in mild frustration.

"But that's what happens sometimes when you're being led by God and I really think you are." "It's unusual what you're doin' but it's not the first time that this has happened, it's just your first time."

"And I think that it's time for me to stop talkin' and get busy with it and I'll let you know how it goes."…

September 4
Friday

"This is nothin' but the work of God and I don't know whether he did this on purpose out of spite or what he was thinkin'." Frances remarked Friday afternoon as she and Michael sat out on the deck. "I don't understand why he didn't tell me about these and if you hadn't been down there lookin' for paper work, we might not have ever known about it."

"I was thinkin' about this before I left work this mornin' and he might've told Paul and maybe he forgot all about it." Michael said after a moment.

"There's just one way to find out huh?" She asked him as she continued to examine the documents. "And he just waved at me half an hour ago when he got home from wherever he went so I know he's home over there."

"Want me to text him and have him come over here?" Michael asked her as he became increasingly curious.

"Do what you do honey because I can tell you're not gonna leave it alone are you?" She asked him, amused.

"You know me don't you?" He asked her as he began texting on his phone. "I think you do."

"This is news to me, I don't know anything about this." Paul remarked fifteen minutes later after sitting down with them.

"Then I guess we'll never know why he wanted to hide this then but like I said before, if you hadn't gone down there for those other papers, we might not have ever found out about this." Frances said. "And like I said before, this is a God thing."

"We need to get to the bank and Michael, I think we need to let you know that Janice is entitled to whatever these are worth too." Paul told him. "I feel like I can speak for the rest of us when I say that."

"Of course she is, she's just as much his as the rest of you are and if anybody has a problem with that, send 'em to me, please and thank-you." Frances said.

"I think you know your kids better than that mother, don't even give that another thought."

"I'm just coverin' my tracks and I'm not sayin' a word about this until we find out exactly what we're workin' with." She said as she noticed James pull up in the driveway.

"There's your girl man, I heard that you're about ready to do your thing." Paul said to Michael as Janice slowly got out of the car.

"Word gets around huh?"

"You know it does but you're marryin' into this family and I think you know by now, we've got your back."

"I'm ridin' with James again so Marie can use my car and turn the rental car back in, that was gettin' expensive." Janice remarked half an hour later as she and Michael sat down at the picnic table between the two houses. "And I'm not comfortable anymore tryin' to drive anyway so she might as well have it for a minute." She added as she started to peel an orange.

"Are you ready for what's about to happen to you?" He asked her with genuine concern.

"I think I am." "When I went to the doctor last week, he said everything looked okay, she's in the right position and all of that stuff I didn't even know about." She said. "Chris has been explainin' a lot to me but she said I won't really know what she's talkin' about until I go through it myself."

"You know I can't wait to see her don't you?"

"Really?" She asked, a little surprised.

"You're still worried about that aren't you?" He asked as he reached into his shirt pocket for the ring box.

"I'm really tryin' not to be because I don't want you to think that I don't trust you." She truthfully admitted.

"Will this help a little with that?" Michael asked her as he opened it up for her to see.

At that, she could say nothing but stare at the set of rings that she had previously stored in her mind for future reference, before she allowed her tears to come.

"Are you serious?" She managed to say after a moment.

"Yes ma'am I am." He immediately answered. "And I know that this doesn't prove that much but it's a start." He told her. "I know that we still have a long way to go but I want you to have somethin' that you can actually see to keep you reminded that I'm serious." He continued.

She nodded then as he started taking the engagement ring out of the box. "So can I put this on your finger?" He asked her as he felt his emotions rise, along with a feeling of assurance that he was making the right move.

She nodded again, too overcome to speak as he gently slipped the ring on her left hand. To her, it was an unbelievable moment after the turbulence that she had experienced for the majority of her young life.

"This is to thank you for givin' me another chance because I know now that I gave you a bad first impression of me." Michael told her then. "But God knew what He was doin' and He doesn't do things half way so this is my way of startin' to prove myself to you." He added with a spirit of love and sincerity that she was able to feel.

"This doesn't feel real but I know it is."

"It is real and if you wanna make me happy about this, I don't want you to doubt God for one thing because if it weren't for Him, this wouldn't have come together like it has." He told her. "I want you to let go of your doubts about it, and I know that we're gonna have problems like everybody else but this is gonna be okay sweetheart."…

September 6
Sunday

"I was at work the other day and it just came to me out of nowhere Douglas." Sheila told him Sunday afternoon after dinner in the family room. "But I feel like I have to run this by you first because it's about you." She said cautiously, waiting on his reaction.

"Am I in trouble?" He asked her.

"No you're not in trouble but I'm feelin' like I need to write a book about you and I already have the title in my mind."

He didn't answer but waited for her to continue.

"How does "From Junkyard to Jesus" sound to you?" She asked him after a moment.

"How come you're just now tellin' me that you're a writer ma'am?" He asked her, steering the conversation away from himself.

"I don't really consider myself a writer." She said after a moment. "But after what happened a couple of weeks ago with Aunt Katherine when she heard your testimony in there, I can't just sit on that." She added, shaking her head.

"So are you askin' me for my permission to do that?" He asked her.

"Sort of kind of and I had thought about just doin' it without sayin' anything but that didn't seem right, you know what I mean?"

"Were you gonna surprise me or somethin'?"

"That was my first idea but I wouldn't have been able to get my content without you."

"Let me ask you this." He said then.

"Uh oh."

"Sheila Scott, you know better, you don't have anything to be afraid of, this is me." He said, assuring her. "But is this your idea or somethin' that you feel like the Lord is leadin' you to do?"

"At first I thought that it was just me but you know how somethin' will nag at you and won't leave you alone?" She asked him.

"You know I do and it never fails if you're sensitive enough to your spirit."

"I mean I tried to tell myself that I'm not anybody's author but when I do this, it's gonna be God writin' through me because this just isn't me." She said, shrugging a little.

"Then if you feel that way, who am I to stop you?" He asked her. "But what do you want from me?"

"If I can just get you to put on paper about how you got that Junkyard name, that would be a start." She began "And if you don't feel comfortable doin' that, I understand but this is for the sake of souls and that's what counts." "I know that's what matters the most to you too because I've seen you in action sir." She told him.

"In action?" He asked her out of curiosity.

"I know that it's the Lord that saves people but when you see stuff like what happened with Andre' that night, that was just an example of what I need to get out there." She said. "I mean what we saw that night is what people need to know about and if you hadn't been there to do what the Lord had you to do, he probably wouldn't have the testimony that he has." She finished with heartfelt conviction.

"But what that proves is that you can't go by what you see in people." Douglas said. "But God knows the heart and He led him there because He knew that he was ready and it didn't take long for it to happen."

"Would you be willin' to explain what went on from what you remember about it?"

"Definitely because there's a lot of Andre's out there that need to know that there's help from God for the asking." He said after a moment. "And it was because of the way that those two brothers worked with me for that seven days that lit a fire in me to be there for souls because that's all that counts in the long run."

"And there's somethin' about you that reminds me so much of Paul on his way to Damascus." She said, anticipating his reaction.

"I've heard that before and the difference between us is that he thought he was doin' the right thing by wastin' the church." He began. "I was doin' all the wrong things on purpose and lovin' it but the Lord knew what it would take to get my attention and as horrible as it was, it was the experience that woke me up big time."

"So if I do this, would you be willin' to describe what happened?"

"It wouldn't be my favorite thing to do but if it would help somebody else, it would be worth it." He said. "I wouldn't have to go into any gory details but the point needs to made that life is fragile and it's a vapor." "You can be here one minute and the next, you're in eternity and you can't be gamblin' about where that is, bottom line."

"And that's your whole passion in other words?"

"I can't get away from it and we hear about bein' ready for the rapture or the comin' of the Lord, however you wanna say it, but what if you go to bed one night and don't wake up the next mornin'?"

"That's your personal rapture huh?"

"If you have your house in order it is but if is a big word." He said. "There's not a day that goes by that I don't think about that because nothin' else really matters in the long run." He emphasized. "And I'm not gonna go knockin' on somebody's door and try to force salvation on anybody because the Lord knows how to put people in your path that are ready for truth."

"Andre'?"

"Exactly, and I had no idea that we were gonna come face to face with one of the guys that almost killed Terry that night." He said as he recalled the trauma that she had suffered. "But somewhere along the line, he found some remorse behind all of that and God led him to a place where he could get his help."

"That whole thing was just so awesome to me and that's what I'm gonna be tryin' to describe in this book if I can get it together."

"Some things you can't really describe because until you experience it yourself, there just aren't any words." He told her. "And I know that's not news to you but if you feel like that this is the Lord leadin' you to do this, I'll do what I can to help you with it." He added as Terry came in with a plate.

"It's startin' to rain so we had to come in." She said as she, Michael and Marie sat down at the table across from the fireplace.

"Did you tell him Sheila?" Terry asked her.

"Did I tell you Douglas?" Sheila asked him.

"Yes ma'am she told me but I don't want anybody thinkin' that I'm in this for any kind of fame or fortune, that's not what it's about."

"C'mon Douglas, we know you better than that."

"I hope so but I had to clairify that anyway." "I can't assume anything and if you do make any profit from it, don't feel like any of it has to come this way, it's all yours."

"But that's not why I'm doin' it, money is not the point." She began. "I'm doin' it because I think more people need to know that there's help from God if they want it and this is just my way of gettin' it out there."

"Then that sounds like to me that you have a burden for souls that all of us are supposed to have, and if you think I can help you with that, then let's go for it."

"Do you ever see any of those people that you used to run around with?"

"Sometimes I do, I was at the barbershop the other day and a guy that I used to roll the dice with all night long came in there in a wheelchair and one leg." He said after thinking a moment. "I recognized him before he knew who I was and by the way he looked, I could tell how much the world had chewed him up and spit him out." He continued. "But it's things like that, that help me to never forget where I came from and how faithful God is."

"Because that could've been you." Sheila said.

"Or worse because the way I was actin' like a fool out of my mind, I can almost guarantee you, I'd be long gone." He said as his emotions began to rise to the surface. "And before I got out of there, he asked me to go to the back room with him for some prayer he said." "That was the last thing that I expected to hear but you never know what kind of an Impact you're havin' on people so you have to keep yourself in check."

"Are you takin' notes Sheila?" Michael asked her as "Nita brought Annette in and gave her to Douglas.

"Irene said she won't go to sleep for anybody but you so here you are sir." She said as he laid her on his chest. "So Michael, I like that rock that you put on Janice's finger, when's the big day?"

"We don't know yet, it might be another six months but I feel better because she knows now that I haven't been just talkin', you know what I mean?"

"I knew that, she told me the same thing so I was just checkin' to make sure you're on the same page."

"Yeah we are and I don't want her feelin' any kind of pressure to do anything right now except get ready for the baby because things just aren't gonna be the same." He said as he opened a can of pop.

"And I'll be glad when she drops that load because she's keepin' me up at night." "She said she can't get comfortable anymore so it's gettin' close, yay."

"But that's when the real fun starts, when she comes home with her, she'll be up probably two or three times a night." Marie told her.

"And she'll be in her own space too, she's movin' in the nursery from the start so I can dream in peace." 'Nita said as she sat down next to Terry. "She got another text from Miss what's her face too last night, did she tell you?"

"Yeah she told me but that woman is not gonna run anything that has to do with what's goin' on, it's not happenin'." He said with determination. "I know that she wants to be around when she's born and all of that but there's a way to do it." He added. "And after that message today, nothin' or nobody is gonna take my peace because I've got right on my side."

"I just happened to notice Janice when they put the title up on the monitor and she just kind of lost it, it hit the spot." Sheila said.

"What was it, "Your Perfect Peace?" Terry asked her.

"That's what it was." Michael said. "I ordered the D.V.D. because I need to hear that one over and over again, it hit the spot big time." He added, agreeing with her.

"So what's the plan, are you gonna flip Aunt France's old house into your dream forever mansion?"

"It probably won't be forever but we'll be there for awhile." "We went on a walk through yesterday and she let me know how she wants things so she's the boss as far as that goes."

"Then when you have fifty million kids in a few years, you can build you a new house and live happily ever after 'til Jesus comes, right?"

"One day at a time, I'm doin' things slow and steady because I don't need any setbacks."

"But you know that crazy woman is gonna try to mess things up for you so you need to have a plan in place."

"And I love you too 'Nita Scott, try not to worry about it." He told her, determined not to get caught up in a useless conversation. "So what time are you leavin' for the airport?" He asked Marie, quickly changing the subject.

"In about an hour." She said, glancing at her watch. "He's supposed to get here around six-thirty." She added, referring to Jerry."He's stayin' with Randy and Donna and I might end up there before he goes back because Miss Florence has pretty much taken things over with mother."

"And both of 'em are lovin' it, that's the crazy part about it." "They just clicked." Sheila remarked.

"They clicked because that whole thing was set up by the Lord." She said. "I remember the first time that I talked to her on the phone when she was askin' me if it was okay for her to talk to her." Marie commented. "So I don't have a problem with it, whatever works."

"Am I in trouble or somethin'?" Janice asked after walking over to Paul and Jane's house with Chris and Irene.

"Why would you be in trouble honey, don't be paranoid." Irene told her. "And I love your ring, this is the first time I've seen it up close." She said as she lifted her left hand.

"Me too, and he totally shocked me, I didn't really think this would happen so soon."

"Did you cry?"

"You know I did, we were sittin' right there at the picnic table and I had no idea, I thought we were just goin' for a walk." She said as they approached it."

"And he just sprung it on you huh?"

"He did and I sat over there and lost it like a big baby."

"You don't have to apologize for that, you have the right." Chris told her. "And now's the time to start plannin' stuff because you're not gonna have the time or the energy in a few weeks, so start now."

"You got over here just in time didn't you?" Frances said five minutes later, right before the heavy rain began. as they walked in from the patio to the kitchen where Paul and Donna sat at the table waiting on them.

"What's happenin'?" Janice cautiously asked as she began to remember the day in April that had been so painful.

"Honey it's okay, you looked scared." Paul told her as she slowly sat down. "And what it is, we called you over here because we found out about some money that we didn't know we had and it's just fair for you to be a part of this."

"From where?" She asked after a moment, confused.

"Michael found some papers that William had stuck in a file cabinet down in the basement." Frances began. "He took out four C.D.s in their names thirty years ago and he didn't tell me a thing about it."

"What's that?" She timidly asked for fear of appearing "unlearned."

"That's short for certificates of deposits and it's like a savings account that you open that earns interest over time." Paul began. "It's better than a regular savings account because it pays you more interest than a bank will." "So what he did was put a hundred dollars in four separate accounts and that money sat there for thirty years and it's way more than a hundred dollars now, believe me when I tell you."

"So we decided that since he was as much your father as he was ours that you should get a part of what we got." Irene told her as Paul slid an envelope across the table to her.

"Are you serious?" Janice asked in complete shock as she stared at it as if afraid to open it.

"Yes ma'am we're serious, we didn't think it was right to leave you out of this just because of the way things happened." Chris told her.

She nodded a little as she started to slowly open the envelope that contained a check for five thousand dollars, made out to her, signed by Paul.

"This is crazy." Janice said through tears a moment later." "I was just down prayin' this mornin' about wantin' to pay my car off before I have to go on maternity leave." She managed to say through her awe of God and His ability to do more than what she could ask or think.

"Then you have another testimony that the Lord answers prayer." Donna told her, as her tears became contagious.

"I just wasn't expectin' anything like this and it's almost exactly what I needed." She continued.

"But when you're trustin' God honey, there's no limits to what He'll do for you." Frances told her. "And He knows exactly when to work because just think about it." She continued. "Those papers sat down there in that file cabinet for thirty years and it wasn't an accident that Michael went down there and found 'em so it was just time."

"So that's one more thing that you won't have to worry about." Paul told her. "And since all five of us came from the same guy, we felt like you shouldn't be left out of this so just thank God and let's keep it movin'."

At that, she nodded in agreement before speaking again. "Is just thank you enough?" She asked them then.

"Consider it done."

"Do you think Douglas would mind if I gave this to him to do?" She asked Irene. "I don't know how all of that works."

"All you have to do is sign it, then give it to him and he'll take it to the bank where your loan is and pay it off." She told her.

"And he'll be glad to do it, you don't need to be worried about that part of it."

"Then you'll get your title and that's one less thing you'll have to worry about." Paul said. "Keep the oil changed every three months and it's all good.".

"Is this the same place?" Jerry asked two hours later as Donna opened the door to he and Marie.

"It is, can you tell somebody else lives here now?" She asked him as he looked around, recalling the last time he was there.

"We're still workin' on it but it's better than it was a couple of months ago." Donna said as they followed her into the kitchen.

"So you bought this place from Chris and her husband huh?"

"Yep we did, he grew up in this house and he bought it from his parents about twenty five years ago so we kept it in the family."

"They don't make 'em like this anymore." He remarked, looking around. "I remember the last time I was sittin' in here, the stuff was hittin' the fan wasn't it?" He asked, maliciously reminding Marie of what had happened months before.

"Yeah it was but that's behind me and I'm not goin' back there." She told him. "You brought back a lot of stuff didn't you?" She asked Donna, anxious to change the subject.

"We always do, I won't have to cook til Tuesday or Wednesday." She said as she handed Jerry a styrofoam plate from the counter.

"So I get to taste the food from the country huh?" He asked as he began to fill it a moment later.

"You do, they start cookin' on Saturday because stuff tastes better the second day."

"I might have to go out there and check it out before I head back to D.C.". He continued as he spooned potato salad on his plate before he suddenly grabbed his chest in pain and fell to the floor.

"Randy had just walked in there and they told me if he hadn't done the C.P.R. thing with him he wouldn't have made it here." Marie remarked an hour later at the E.R. waiting room area with Frances and Douglas.

"And I'm guessin' this is why I was down on my knees prayin' this mornin' and he came to my mind." Frances began . "I knew he'd be here today and this must be the reason why the Lord got some prayer from me for what we're lookin' at now." She continued, reassuring her that the situation was under control.

"Are you serious Aunt Frances?" She asked her in total surprise.

"I knew he'd be here today and I couldn't rest until I made sure that he was covered." She began. "None of us knew that this was comin' but nothin' takes God by surprise and I learned with this man right here how to be obedient to the voice of God." She added as she touched Douglas on his arm.

Marie nodded in agreement then, while allowing the Lord help her keep her from "falling apart." "And I can't believe how quick all of this happened, he was fixin' a plate and he grabbed his chest and fell out and Randy had just walked in, I'm not kiddin' you." She finished in amazement as she thought about how God had orchestrated the circumstances.

"And that should help you to know that this is not the end of this story." Frances told her. "Don't you allow fear to overtake your mind because that doesn't do anything but torment you and that's just not acceptable." She added with authority.

"But I keep thinkin' about what probably would've happened if he hadn't come in there like he did." She responded.

"But honey he did and if today had been his day to leave here, nothin' could've stopped it." Douglas told her. "The prayer that she sent up for him this mornin' might've saved his life so just concentrate on that." He added. "But I have another question for you."

"I know, I can tell by the way you look like you're in deep thought over there." Marie said as she managed to laugh a little.

"So you know me a little huh?"

"I think I know what you're gonna ask me and I wish I could put into words how frustrated I've been with him."

"You're probably feelin' that way because you know what God can do to help him and he doesn't wanna go there does he?"

"I keep tellin' him that the Lord can deliver him from havin' to smoke three packs of cigarettes a day and he tells me not to worry about it because he can quit anytime he wants to."

"And that's the way you think you feel but in your gut, you know that's not the way it is." Douglas said as he recalled his own addiction.

"His blood pressure has been through the roof but nothin' seems to get his attention." She continued as she took a tissue from a nearby box, right before an E.R. physician approached them.

"Mrs. Kennedy?" He asked as he sat down next to her.

She nodded. "What's goin' on?"

"I'm Dr. Upshaw and let me begin by saying that your husband is a very lucky man." He continued. "We were told by one of the E.M.T.'s that brought him in that someone had given him the C.P.R. procedure before they got there and if that hadn't happened, he wouldn't be here without a doubt."

At that, Marie reacted with thanks and praise to God through cautious tears of relief.

"He's not out of the woods by any means, let me make that clear to you." He continued. "We did a heart scan and he has two blocked arteries that caused the attack and he's going to need surgery if he expects to recover from this."

"How soon?" Marie asked him.

"As soon as possible, we don't have a lot of time to waste." He said without hesitation. "He's going to need a couple of stents in the affected arteries and he should be able to recover if he takes care of himself."

"So you're sayin' that this'll happen tonight sometime?" Douglas asked him.

"As soon as we get a signed consent, we need to get this done." He emphasized. "Right now, we have him sedated and of course he's on a heart monitor and you can go in to see him if you like before he has surgery." He concluded as he stood up.

"Honey you go with him to sign the paper and we'll meet you in there." Frances told Marie after she and Douglas instinctively "rose to the occasion", knowing that the fervent prayer of the righteous avails much.

"Okay." She managed to say as she got a text from Janice, informing her that she and Michael were on the way there.

"He wasn't havin' any warnin' signs or anything before he went down?" Michael asked an hour later in the waiting area with Marie and Janice.

She shook her head. "If he was, he never told me about it and I just hope this is enough to make him quit smokin.'" She continued after a moment. "And I can't wait to talk to Randy; I mean he didn't stop to think about it, he just acted like it was somethin' he does everyday." She added as she recalled the scene in her mind.

"Did he just happen to walk in the kitchen when it happened?"

"It was like it was on cue, almost like he knew what was about to happen." Marie said, still trying to figure it all out.

"Did they let you go back there to see him before they took him to surgery?" Janice asked her.

"I went to sign the consent form, then when I went in the I.C.U. room to see him, Douglas and Aunt Frances had just finished doin' what they do best and I could just feel the power of God all in there."

Does he know what's goin' on?" Michael asked her.

"He's been sedated since they got him here so as far as he knows, he'll just wake up and it'll be done." She said as she looked up and noticed Randy step off the elevator.

"Donna told me to come out here and I hope I'm not gettin' in the way." He said as he approached them.

"Are you kiddin' me?" Marie asked him as she reached out to hug him. "I just got through tellin' them that I couldn't wait to talk to you." She added as he sat down a moment later.

"How is he?" Was his first question out of genuine concern.

"His doctor told me that he has two blocked arteries so he's in surgery, they're puttin' a couple of stents in his heart." She began. "And he also said that if he hadn't had the C.P.R. that you did, he just wouldn't be here." She continued as she got more tissues.

"And you know what?" He asked then. "They made us take a first aid course on my job and that was part of the trainin.'" He said. "If we didn't pass this twenty hour course, we couldn't keep drivin' our routes."

"Are you serious?"

"I'm serious, and that was just two weeks ago so it was still pretty fresh in my mind about what to do." He said with an obvious humble spirit about him. "But I didn't really think that I would ever have to go there and when I think about it, it wasn't anything but the Lord that kept me from just freezin' up, I'm serious."

"And I was just tellin' them that it was like it was somethin' that you do everyday." Marie told him.

"It was just one of those things where you're in the right place at the right time so just thank God that it worked out that way." He concluded. "Did they say how long he'd be in surgery?"

"It's probably gonna be two or three hours and I appreciate you comin' out here but don't feel like you have to stay."

"I got orders from Donna to do what I have to do and I feel like I need to be here." He told her.

"We'll be back, I'm goin' on a tour." Michael said then as he helped Janice stand up.

"We'll be here but don't go far." Marie told them.

"So did Donna tell me that he has some relatives that live here?" Randy asked her a moment later.

"His step-mother lives on the east side somewhere but I don't have her phone number." She said after thinking about it. "He might have it in his phone but they haven't given me any of his stuff yet."

"You're not scared of this are you?"

"I'm really tryin' to let the Lord help me not to be and when I think about what might've happened if you hadn't come in there, it's really kind of blowin' my mind."

"But you have to know that if it had been his time to check out of here, it wouldn't have happened the way it did." He told her. "And that makes me think about the day that I picked up a regular rider on my route." He began. "He would be there like clockwork and get off at the same stop everyday and when I stopped to let him off and he wasn't comin' to the front, I looked in the mirror to see where he was, and he was still in his seat." "It looked like he had dozed off and one of the other passengers yelled at me and told me that he was dead back there and I needed to stop and take care of it."

"Are you serious?" "How long ago was this?" Marie asked, fascinated.

"This was a couple of years ago and this guy wasn't even fifty years old and sat on my bus and died on the spot." He said, shaking his head.

"And he didn't seem sick or anything?"

He shook his head. "When he got on that day, he told me that he had just about saved enough money for a down payment on a car and he wouldn't have to be takin' the bus anymore and ten minutes later, he was gone." "It was crazy but what that experience did for me was point up how fragile all of us are and you just can't gamble about where you're goin' when you leave here."

"I'm tryin' to understand why this happened here and not at home but it's startin' to make sense now."

"It does and when things settle down, we'll know why." He answered as he noticed Kathrine and Florence approach them from a nearby escalator."

"Since when can you be on an escalator?" Marie asked her in surprise.

"We started to get on the elevator then I decided that I would try it and it worked." Kathryn said as she slowly sat down next to Marie. "Me and the Lord got it done."

"So I see." "And thanks for comin' out here, I wasn't expectin' all of this." She told Florence.

"We wouldn't have it any other way, and the more people that you have around you, the better off you'll be dear." She said as she sat down next to Kathryn. "And do you mind telling us what happened?"

"I picked him up at the airport and when we got to Randy and Donna's house, he started fixin' a plate in the kitchen and just fell out." She said, shaking her head. "He grabbed his chest and hit the floor and I know this had to be the Lord." She added as she recalled the moment again in her mind, as she became emotional at the thought of what had transpired. "Randy walked in there right before he passed out and it was like it had all been rehearsed or somethin'." She said through her tears. "He got down to where he was and did the C.P.R. thing like he did it everyday and that just had to be God." She said again, careful to give Him the glory.

"Oh my, don't you just love the way He does things?" Florence asked her as she began to identify with her. "How long have you known how to do that?" She asked Randy.

"A couple of weeks but this is not about me, we need to start thankin' God that he's still here and what we have to do to keep helpin' him when he comes out of this."

"I just wanted to get some kind of idea of where you're gonna be because I know I won't have any business up here." Michael remarked as he and Janice slowly walked toward the L.D.R. unit on the third floor.

"They give you a tour when you're thirty six weeks or more and I was shocked." She said . "I didn't have any idea that there were so many monitors and machines and stuff that they hook you up to when you're in labor."

"So have you talked to Chris about all of that stuff?"

"She told me about how James passed out when Stephen was born; he didn't have any idea that it would be so graphic." She added, laughing at the thought.

"He never told me that, I'm gonna have to ask him how that happened." He said as they approached the nursery where three babies were there in plain view.

"It's still kind of hard to believe that this is gonna be me in a couple of weeks." Janice said a few moments later as they watched a nurse bathe a newborn.

"You're not sorry about this are you?"

"I'm sort of scared but I'm not sorry and when I think about it, I just needed somebody to tell me not to do what I was about to six or seven months ago." She said, shaking her head a little. "And it just happened to be Douglas that told me that wasn't an option and I'm so glad I listened." She said as she let a tear come down her face.

"So that's how it all started with him?"

" It was somethin' about him that made me comfortable with lettin' it all out, you know what I mean?" "I had only known him for two or three weeks but I could tell that he really cared about what I was goin' through and that's helped me to be the same way with other people."

"I guess that's part of what love is huh?" He asked after a moment as they continued to watch the work of the trained caregivers.

"It is and this time last year, it was all about me and what I wanted because I didn't really know how to love anybody else." She said, shaking her head at the very thought.

"I asked him one time about how he's been able to see you as one of his own daughters." He began. "Then he told me about the day that Aunt Frances sat him down to let him know that he'd probably be the one that you would trust more than anybody else, and he was really reluctant to go there at first."

She nodded. "Irene talked to me about that one day because she wanted me to know that she didn't have a problem with it." She said. "She told me that they had prayed about it and they felt like it was what he needed to do."

"He got the green light from God as Aunt Frances says."

"You don't know how glad I am that he did because I don't think I would've ever known what I missed out on for so long."

"But Kristen's not gonna ever go through what you did so just start lookin' forward to some better days.".

"What am I doin' here?" Jerry asked with a weakened voice just after he woke up after his surgery five hours later, around one-thirty a.m.

"Honey you don't remember what happened?" Marie asked him then as she got up from the nearby chair near his bed.

"What am I doin' here?" He asked again, completely confused, just as his attending nurse walked into the room.

"Mr. Kennedy I need for you calm down for me, your heart can't take any stress right now." She told him as she read his E.K.G. graph. "You suffered a massive heart attack yesterday and from what I hear, you had a family member probably save your life because he knew how to perform C.P.R. on you." She added. "You're a lucky man but it's time for you to rest as much as you can." She concluded as he noticed Marie sitting nearby.

"I don't remember anything." He managed to say, talking directly to Marie.

"You were fixin' your plate and then you just fell on the floor." She told him "And Randy had just walked in and he did what he did; it was nothin' but the Lord that fixed it like that." She added, making sure that he knew where his help had so mercifully come from.

"He said nothing but nodded a little as a single tear came down his face.

"You just had surgery so we don't want you to do anything except rest for right now." The nurse continued. "Two stents were put into the blocked arteries that caused the attack so you have a road ahead that's going to take some time and cooperation from you and the people that love you in order for you to get better."

"Do you have any idea how long he'll be here?" Marie cautiously asked her.

"That's something that you'll have to talk to Dr. Upshaw about and he'll be available tomorrow to fill you in on those details." She concluded as she began to take his blood pressure. "But for right now, he needs to rest before we can begin to determine that."

"I'm findin' out that you don't realize how much you love somebody until you live through a scare like this." Marie remarked around six-thirty with Donna in the kitchen as she fixed breakfast.

"And this should teach all of us how close you can come to leavin' here without even thinkin' about it." Donna said as she started stirring pancake mix for the boys.

"What time does Randy leave for work?"

"His route starts at five so he leaves here around four-thirty but after he got back here from the hospital, he didn't really go to bed, he told me he couldn't sleep."

"I haven't been to bed either but if you don't care, I'm gonna give it a try after I eat somethin'."

"Why would I care Marie, you need to rest so you can be there for Jerry because he's gonna need you more than anybody else." She told her. "And what I can do is take the boys out to the country with Chris and Jane's kids so they won't keep you up."

"I was supposed to take mother for her therapy today too but maybe Florence will do it this once if I ask her."

"You know she will, they're some tight BFFs." She said laughing a little.

"What would I do without you guys?" She asked her then as she thought about the support that she experienced.

"But this is just the start, it might be a while before things start to feel normal again." Donna said after a moment. "And I'm not sayin' that to discourage you but I'm just keepin' it real because that's how we overcome stuff."

"By dealin' with it head on huh?"

"You got it and Randy told me last night after he got back from the hospital, that he feels like Jerry is on his heart now and nothin' is gonna stop him from helpin' him through this."

"If he can talk to him about gettin' his soul together, then the rest of it would fall into place." Marie said. "And it might be different with him if another guy talks to him because I've gotten nowhere fast when it comes to that."

"It might seem like that but you never know what's goin' on inside." "As hard core as Douglas was, somethin' got to him and it's no different with Jerry but he has to get the place himself where he knows he's got to make some changes."

"I know, and I've found out that it doesn't make any difference how much I want him to know how much better he'd feel with the Holy Ghost." "He has to want it for himself and I'll never forget how I felt when I finally got the message, somethin' just clicked." She continued. "If it wasn't for Douglas and your mama that broke it down for me, I might've still been out there tryin' to make it on my own."

"Randy told me that they were there prayin' for him before they took him to surgery."

"They were and I don't think they realize how much difference they make when they get together."

"But maybe they do and that might be why they hook up so much." Donna said. "Sheila told me the other day that she's usin' both of 'em in her book and I can't wait to read what she puts together."

"Yeah that's gonna be interesting, I already know." Marie said, obviously distracted by her concern and worry about Jerry.

"What time are you goin' back to the hospital?"

"I need to take a shower and get back over there in a couple of hours." She said after thinking a moment. "And I really hate to be puttin' all of these miles on Janice's car but I really don't have much choice right now."

"I really don't think she's worried about that Marie." "This is an emergency that none of us knew was comin' so don't worry about stuff like that."

"And I've got to call his manager at home to let them know what happened because we don't have any idea when he's gonna be able to get back to D.C." She said as Donna noticed that she was becoming overwhelmed by the whole situation.

"Honey we're not gonna let this beat us, are you listenin' to me?" Donna asked her as she sat down next to her and embraced her as she let her emotions go free.

She nodded a little before speaking. "And I think I might be pregnant on top of all of this."

"But didn't you tell me a couple of months ago that you've been tryin' for a while?" Donna asked after a moment.

"What if I am and he doesn't come out of this?" She asked out of fear of the unknown.

"But what if you are and he does come out of it?" Donna asked. "You can't listen to that kind of stuff when you know that the Lord doesn't give us any more than we can bear." She added as she wiped her own empathetic tears. "Both of us saw what went on in here yesterday and God doesn't do anything halfway, He's giving you a testimony that you won't ever forget."

She nodded then in agreement with her as she reached for a napkin.

"And if you want me to, I can go down the street and get a test for you to take so you'll know one way or another."

"If you don't mind." Marie said, shaking her head a little. "I told him when I picked him up at the airport that I was a couple of weeks late and he just looked at me like I was crazy."

"But if you are, it is what it is and you just have to take it one day a time and keep believin' God." Donna said as she stood back up. "The kids are still sleep and I'll be back before they wake up, give me fifteen minutes."

"I'm not sayin' anything 'til I know he's strong enough to hear it." Marie remarked an hour later after getting a positive result. "This might make him have another attack." She said as she managed to laugh a little.

"No it won't but what you have to do is ask the Lord to keep you calm and not let yourself stress out because that can cause a miscarriage if you're not careful." Donna told her as she started feeding Sarah.

"I guess that I need to start listenin' to people that know

huh?"

"You're gonna be okay and so is Jerry so just be still and know who's in control."..

Chapter 3

September 8
Tuesday

"There he is." Jerry managed to say as Randy walked into his hospital room Tuesday afternoon."

"This is progress, I wasn't expectin' to see you out of bed so .soon." Randy said as they did a quick fist bump.

"They made me get up and sit up so here I am." He said.

"You're lookin' like you're on your way back and I can't tell you how good it is to know that you're gonna be okay." He said with assurance.

"From what they tell me, you get the credit for that man." Jerry said as he felt his emotions begin to "take over."

"I was there because God ordered my steps so I don't get any credit, He showed me what to do so we'll leave it at that." Randy told him. "And this is about you, are they takin' good care of you up here?"

"They're keepin' me doped up so I'm not in any pain." He said after a moment.

"Do you have any idea how long they're gonna keep you here?"

"It'll probably be a couple of weeks and that's scarin' me more than anything."

"But don't let anything stress you out, that's the last thing you need." Randy told him. "And I heard about your news from Marie, how does that make you feel?"

"Man I don't know, that's a lot to process right now." He said, shaking his head. "When she told me, I couldn't believe it but like you said, I'm tryin' not to stress."

"But that's a good thing, you have another reason to get better, you've got to be there for your wife and baby." Randy told him.

"When she told me that man, all I wanted to do was grab a smoke but I know that can't happen anymore if I wanna keep livin', right?"

"I think you're gettin' it and we know that it's gonna take a lot of help but we want you to know how much the Lord can do for you if you let Him."

"Yeah you're soundin' like Marie now, she's been tellin' me that for months." He said with an air of skepticism.

"She's tellin' you that because she loves you and she knows what it means to be delivered from things, you know what I mean?"

"But she's never had a cigarette in her life so she really can't relate man, see where I'm comin' from?"

"I understand why you'd think that but let's just take one thing at a time." Randy said then. "Nobody is gonna put any pressure on you to do anything but we just wanna see you up and out of here."

"I was goin' through his suitcase and I found this." Marie said with Douglas and Irene, out on the screened porch around six-thirty. "And I'm not throwin' stones but I figured you'd know." She added as she handed him a small plastic bag containing a white powdery substance.

"Don't worry about that, I'm over it." He said as he took it from her. "Since I've had a couple of sessions with Sheila about this book she's writin', I have to remember that this is not about me."

"It's about who might pick her book up and read about what you went through."

"Exactly and if I have to go back in time to help somebody else get over, it's worth it." He said. "And yeah, this is what you think it is." He added as he set the small bag down. "But what we don't want you to do is panic, this is gonna be okay." He assured her.

"I keep hearin' that from everybody and I know what God can do when your faith is right." She began. "And I'm really tryin' to get to the place where you and Aunt Frances are but it's gonna be a while before I get there, I'm serious." She said with an air of brutal honesty.

"But you have to remember that we've had to go through some things and that's where you are right now." He told her. "This might look bad but I think both of us know that there isn't anything that God can't do but at the same time, he's gonna have to come to himself and know how much he needs the help of God, bottom line." "We can want that for him but it's got to come from the cry of his soul and when he gets hungry enough, things'll start to happen."

"He's been to church with me a couple of times and he couldn't wait for it be over so he could go outside and light up and it's just crazy how those things can trap a person."

"And I know where he is." Douglas said. "When the devil is on your trail tryin' to take you out, you're helpless." He said as he recalled his own experience. "And nobody can convince me otherwise that it wasn't the prayers of people that I didn't even know that were preservin' me before I finally came to myself."

"I don't know what it might take for him but if this doesn't wake him up, I don't know what will."

"Nobody knows his heart except the Lord and what you can't do is give him the impression that you better do this or that because sometimes, that has the opposite effect."

"Believe me, there's a lot of truth to that one." Irene remarked. "I would do things on purpose to make my point that I didn't wanna hear none of it, leave me alone, I get it." "I knew that I needed the Holy Ghost and was mad and offended that he went and did what he did." She continued as they laughed at her."

"But one day Paul came across town and said some stuff to me that finally got my attention and the rest is history as they say."

"And that's not what works with him so I'm takin' one thing at a time."

"What you do is love him to God and watch Him do the rest." Douglas told her. "I've seen it happen too many times, and this stuff right here is what you do when you're cryin' out because there's a void there that needs to be taken care of." He added as picked up the bag again in disgust and tossed it back on the table in front of him.

"Is it somethin' that I'm doin' or not doin'?" She asked as she began to blame herself.

"Don't go there because that's exactly what your adversary the devil wants you to think." "You can be the best husband or wife in the world but that doesn't satisfy the soul and that's what this is about."

"Can you tell me why you and Aunt Frances have all the answers?" She asked him after a moment.

"We don't but it's just a matter of goin' through things and learnin' what works and what doesn't." He said. "And this experience that you're dealin' with now is gonna turn out for your good even if it feels like the bottom is fallin' out of everything right now."

"So when he found out that he's gonna be a daddy, what was his reaction?" Irene asked her.

"Like I told Donna, it was like he didn't believe it but I refuse to get caught up in that because time is gonna prove it."

"That's it, don't let anything or anybody take your peace of mind and just know that the Lord wouldn't have allowed this if you weren't able to get through it." Douglas told her. "Just be still and let us help you sort all of this out because some things can be too much all at once."

"Do they have any idea how long he's gonna be in the hospital?" Irene asked her.

"I talked to his doctor this mornin' and it'll probably be at least a week and that depends on how much he cooperates." Marie said after a moment. "He has a really tough stubborn streak and most of the time it's his way or no way and this is gonna really rub him the wrong way."

"You mean he doesn't like to be told what he can or can't do huh?"

"Exactly." She said, agreeing with her. "And most guys don't but this is really gonna be a challenge for him, I already know."

"But if he wants to get up off of his back, he really doesn't have much choice." Douglas remarked. "And the best thing for you to do is ask the Lord to give you the wisdom to deal with him." "You're the one that has the most influence on him and you're the one with greater spirit so you have the advantage." He continued. "Don't allow any spirit of fear to overtake you because that's how you lose your victory and I could go on and on but some things you have to experience yourself to get it, you know what I mean?"

"You can go on as long as you want to because you don't know how much it's helpin' me to hear you talk to me like this." She said as she got a tissue from the box on the table.

"God knows what it takes to strengthen you and later on at some point, you'll be able to tell somebody else how faithful He is." He continued. "It might look a little rough right now but when you get to place where you can say Lord your will be done, nothin' is gonna defeat you."

She nodded before speaking again then. "We had some Sunday school lessons about that at home a couple of months ago, and that's really not easy to do unless the Lord is helpin' you to get there."

"And that's because we get so used to dependin' on our own minds and how we think things should be handled but God sees the big picture." Douglas said. "And the bottom line to all of this is the weapon and power of our prayers with this." "You're not in this by yourself so whatever it takes, you're gonna come out ahead." He said, right before he received a text message from Janice.

"She called about half an hour ago and she wanted me to give her your number and I thought, no way." Janice remarked a minute later on the phone, referring to Mary Ann.

"Did she say why?"

"She said that she needs to talk to you and she got really upset because I wouldn't give it to her without askin' you first."

"You did the right thing so don't worry about that and it's not that I won't talk to her but there's a way to do things. He told her. "Is she back in D.C.?"

"She didn't say where she was but she kept sayin' that she has to talk to you because she hasn't been able to sleep because of what happened when she was here."

"So did it sound like she was blamin' me for that?" He asked her, becoming amused but concerned at the same time.

"It was sort of like she wanted to but she was afraid to come out and say it."

"I'll tell you what." He began after a moment. "Send me her number and I'll call her." "I'll let Irene know what's goin' on and use the land line because I don't feel comfortable with her havin' my cell." He concluded. "Does that sound like a plan?"

"How come I didn't think about that?"

"Probably because I've been around a bit longer than you have and I know people a little better too but I don't want you to worry about this." He told her. "Just stay prayerful and I'll let you know how it goes."

"Negro I'm layin' awake at night just tryin' to figure you out because I've never come across anything like what happened the last time I saw you." Mary Ann remarked with Douglas on the phone, half an hour later. "That scared the you know what out of me and I need to know some things before I come back."

"And before you come back, I want you to understand that you don't need to be afraid of me or anybody else here." "That's number one, that's not what I'm about." He emphasized. "But what you do need to know is that you're dealin' with people that stay in touch with the Lord and we don't mean you any harm but there are some things that we can't tolerate."

"Who told you that I was carryin' a gun, that's what's blowin' my mind." She admitted to him.

"I'll put it like this." He began. "Let's just say that God sees and knows everything and we'll leave it at that because if I went into the details, you might not believe it anyway." He said after a moment.

"So you're tellin' me that God told you that I had that gun in my bag?"

"How else would I know that ma'am?" "But what's important now is that it doesn't happen again and it's none of my business where else you carry it, but when it comes to situations like the day you were here, we can't have it." He finished with the voice of authority.

"I have a permit if that makes any difference to you." She said after a moment.

"I know all about that, I used to carry a permit and a gun too but that doesn't have anything to do with what we're dealin' with now." He told her. "And I hope this clears up some stuff because you shouldn't be losin' sleep because of it."

"Why should that matter to you?"

"It matters because I don't want to be responsible for that kind of issue, you know what I mean?" He asked her. "I've been there and it's no joke so I can relate, and it's a good thing that you got in touch with me because I think you understand now what went on."

"I need you to do me a favor and make sure that I know the minute Janice goes into labor." She told him a moment later. "I will be there and I don't want anybody to try to stop me." She added with determination.

"There's no reason for anybody to try to stop you, we know that this baby is your granddaughter and you have the right to be around." "But there's a way to do it without startin' any trouble, so when we know the baby is comin' we'll let you know."…

September 11
Friday

"It's been almost a week and they're tellin' us now that he needs to be in rehab for another two so that's where we are now." Marie remarked at the table with Donna and Randy Friday afternoon.

"So does he have a problem with that?" Randy asked as he started to feed Sarah.

"He says he's feelin' better and just wants to get back home but they won't release 'til they see that he's makin' some kind of progress. Marie said. "Then on top of that, he drops this bombshell on me by sayin' he's not a hundred percent sure that this baby is his."

"Are you serious?" Donna asked.

" I just looked at him and I know that the Lord is helpin' my mouth, you know what I mean?" She said, shaking her head. "I wasn't gonna play into that because I know where it's comin' from and after I sat down with Douglas and Irene, I'm not lettin' anything bring me down."

"Did you get a mini bible class?"

"And you know it." "He has a way of puttin' things into perspective and the two of them have been through some rough days but they're still together and I love it."

"I asked her one time how she felt about the time that he spends with people and she said it wasn't a problem because whenyou're dealin' with the souls of people, that's what it takes." Donna commented.

"And if I thought Jerry would be okay with sittin' down and havin' one of those coversations that you never forget, I might ask him to, no kiddin.'" Marie said after a moment. "I know how he is and I don't wanna do anything that might cause a setback."

"I can see that too but Douglas is the only one in this family that's been where he is and knows what to say or not to say." Randy told her. "And this is not the time to be walkin' on eggshells because we know how close he came to leavin' here."

"Maybe the next time I talk to him, I'll see what he has to say about it but right now, I don't think it would do anything except aggrevate him and make things worse."

"You know him better than anybody else but we cant just sit back and watch him go through when we know what the power of God can do, you know what I mean?" Randy asked her. "This is a matter of lovin' him and his soul so what's more important?"

"Man I was wonderin' when you were gonna make it up here to see me, what's the good word?" Jerry asked around three-thirty as Douglas walked into his room.

"I was in the neighborhood and there was no way I could act like you weren't here." He said as he sat down in a nearby chair. "And you tell me some good news, this is all about you."

"I keep thinkin' that his whole thing is a nightmare that I can't wake up from." He began. "This wasn't supposed to happen man, this is not me." He added, looking around the room in disdain.

"Have they told you how much longer you'll be here?"

"I can't leave 'til I get through this rehab stuff and they're sayin' that could be in a couple of weeks but I can't be here that long."

"What choice do you have?"

"I don't, and that's the bad thing about it." "If it was up to me, I'd get my clothes on and walk out of here and not look back." He answered with an irritable tone.

"But whatever happens, don't ever forget about the mercy of God which is why you're still here." Douglas told him. "It could've gone another way and believe me when I tell you, you had a lifeline and that was for a reason."

"Man don't get me wrong, I'm thankful and all of that but what kind of life am I gonna have when I do get out of here?"

"That has a lot to do with what you're willin' to do so don't let this be a setback for you." "Do you have any idea what God will do for you when you get to the place where you know how much help you need?"

"Now you're soundin' like Marie, did she send you up here?" He asked with a nervous laugh.

"She didn't, I haven't talked to her in a couple of days." Douglas said then. "And I know that Randy's been up here to see you too and we're not here to preach at you or anything close to that but we wanna see you come up out of this." "And at this point, you can't do it by yourself." He concluded with gentle but firm candor.

"If you were anybody else talkin' to me like that, I'd probably tell you to get up outa here." Jerry said after a moment.

" I get that because sometimes it's hard to hear the truth but I saw death happen in 3-D and if it wasn't for the power of God, I'd probably be goin' through some big time P.T.S.D. twenty years later."

"Man that's a long time."

"Tell me about it but when you have the comfort and power of God's spirit, that makes all of the difference." "When my mother-in-law got me on the phone, I was hours away from doin' myself in because I couldn't get that horrible scene out of my head."

Jerry said nothing then as he found himself unaccountably "moved" by the words that he was hearing.

"I think I remember you tellin' me about that back when we were here in April but I was worried about Marie and I probably didn't catch it all."

"Could be. and if she hadn't told me those four little words, I might not be here today." He emphasized, referring to Frances. "She said to let God help me and it worked then and still works today when you get to the place where you know that things are bigger than you, that's when you'll begin to see things change."

"Man I know you that you used to be where I am now so you're probably the only one around here that knows what's goin' on in my head." He said. "And I appreciate you comin' up here but I've got to sort out some stuff and you'll probably be the one that'll hear from me when I get it together."

"Just don't take anything for granted and the more you keep your mind off of your problems and issues, the more God will prove Himself to you."

"Just keep prayin' for me and when I get out of here, you'll be hearin' from me and that's a promise."...

September 13
Sunday

"This girl is about to have my grandchild and I'm not about to be a thousand miles away when it happens." Mary Ann remarked Sunday afternoon with Katherine out on the front porch after "showing up" for dinner.

"I can understand that because that's exactly why I moved but you don't have to worry about us tryin' to keep you away from her." Katherine began. "You're just as much her grandmother as I am but if it starts to be a problem, you might start havin' some issues with Janice and I don't think you want that."

"Where is she anyway?" She asked irritably. "I have a plane to catch back to D.C. and I don't have a lot of time to be waitin' on her."

"She's with Michael, he usually takes her to see what they're doin' with the house he's fixin' up." "She's not gonna have a lot of time after the baby gets here so they're doin' it now."

"Then I need to see it too, where is it?" She demanded.

"Honey I'm leavin' that up to him, it's his house and I don't think he's ready for anybody else to see it yet."

"Why not, has he got somethin' to hide?"

"No he doesn't but it's just not time for him to be bringin' everybody else in there before it's done." Kathryn patiently answered her. "I haven't even seen it so don't feel like it's just you."

"Do you have the address so I can at least see where it is before I leave?" She persisted. "I've got a G.P.S. that works really good so don't think I'll get lost tryin' to find it."

"I still think you should wait 'til they get here, they're probably on their way if you wait a little bit." Kathryn suggested, unswayed by her persistance.

"Well can you call and let him know that they need to hurry up because I need to be at the airport in an hour." She added as Chris came out of the house and motioned Kathryn back in.

"Did you wanna come in and get a plate before you have to go?" She asked her, completely ignoring her demand as she slowly stood up.

"No I'll be right here, waitin' on them to get back here." She said as she began scrolling on her phone.

"How many weeks along are you hon?" An E.M.T. asked Janice in an ambulance after she and Michael were rear ended by a distracted driver as they sat at a red light.

"Almost thirty-eight." She managed to say before whispering the name Jesus for strength and comfort.

"Have you been having contractions at all?" She asked as she began to take her blood pressure.

She nodded before speaking again. "Just a few but they're not regular."

"Well sweetheart, if I had to say, you're probably gonna have your baby in the next twenty-four hours." She said. "Let me see if I can get the heartbeat and we're taking you to the hospital so you can get checked out." "Is that your husband out there talking to the police?" She asked, trying to keep her distracted.

"We're engaged."

"Are you having a girl or boy?"

"It's a girl." Janice said as she inexplicably began to shake uncontrollably.

"It's okay hon, just relax for me." A second technician told her as she raised her blouse to place the stethescope on her. "What's her name?"

"It's Kristen."

"Alright Kristen, we need to hear from you." "Your mommy needs to know that you're okay."

"Have you felt her move or kick since the accident?"

"Maybe a little, it just happened so quick that I haven't really noticed it." Janice said as a spirit of fear tried to overcome her.

"There she is, good baby." The second E.M.T. spoke a few moments later after picking up a strong heartbeat. "It's all good, she sounds like she's in good shape."

"Chris said it just wouldn't have been right for us not to tell her that they're keepin' you and she was right." Marie remarked an hour later with Janice and Kathryn on the L.D.R. floor.

"So where is she now?" She asked referring to Mary Ann.

"She's down in the waitin' area, they're only lettin' two in here at a time so she's on pins and needles right now." Marie answered. "I'm gonna go up and see Jerry so she can come in here for a minute but I'll be back."

"Have you talked to Michael?" Kathryn asked her.

"I had just talked to him right before you got here and he's kind of a mess right now." Janice began. "The guy that hit us doesn't have any insurance and he thinks his car is probably totaled." She added, close to tears.

"Honey you're kiddin.'" Kathryn said said as she handed her a tissue.

She shook her head a little. "He's worried about me and thinks this is his fault because he could've gone another way and I just had to tell him to stop with all of that, we're okay, thank the Lord." She added as she tensed up with an oncoming contraction.

"Do they think the accident made you go into labor?" Marie asked her a minute later.

"It might've but it doesn't really matter, my due date is ten days away." She said as a nurse came in then.

"My dear, I'm gonna check to see if you've dilated any more since you got here." She said as she slipped on exam gloves. "Just relax for me."

"We'll be back, hang in there." Marie told her as she and Kathryn started out the door. "We'll be back."

"Man it's a good thing I prayed before I left this mornin' because it could've been another way." Michael remarked with Douglas on the way to the airport to rent a car. "And I'm findin' out the more that

happens, the quicker we need to make this official." He added, shaking his head. "Do you have any idea how helpless I'm feelin' right now?"

"I've never been where you are but I can see that." Douglas said. "You feel like you need to be there for her but right now, you're limited and you're frustrated, am I right?" He asked him in complete empathy and understanding.

"That's pretty much it in a nutshell and it doesn't have anything to do with takin' her to bed, that's the last thing on my mind right now."

"You went there huh?"

"Man I'm keepin' it real." "She was with me when this happened and I can't be anywhere around her right now and it's workin' on me."

"But what you have to do is make sure she knows that you're not gonna fold up on her just because you're havin' a little bit of a problem here." Douglas told him. "And like you said just a minute ago, this could've been a lot worse but because you acknowledged God before you even left your house this mornin,' you were protected." He added as he pulled over into a parking lot to avoid distractions. "Her and the baby are gonna be okay and as far as your car goes, it happens to the best of us so everything is under control."

"It was two months from bein' paid off but like you said, it happens." Michael said. "And if I remember right, I might have gap insurance on it for stuff like this."

"Check into it because that can make a lot of difference in this whole thing."

"All things are gonna work together for my good huh?"

"I know we say that all of the time but when you learn how to really trust God with things like this, you find out how true that scripture is." He said. "But don't forget the rest of what that says." He continued. "If you love God and are called according to His purpose, it has to work because God can't lie."

"I've found that out too and I'm at the place now where I was when I first got the Holy Ghost; I'm givin' it up, I can't do anything else but believe God."

"And sometimes, He allows things like this to happen to get you there." "If we're not really careful, we can get too independent and start to think that we got this and that's kind of a dangerous place to be."

"I think I've found that out the last couple of months but thanks for the reminder anyway."

"All of us need to be reminded about things like this and goin' through whatever happens will just make you that much stronger." He told him. "Your life is about to change big time and I almost forgot to tell you that your friend Miss Mary Ann is back in town."

"You are kiddin' me man, not this."

"Fraid so and Kathryn told me that she just about ready to head back to D.C. when we found out about your accident, so she made some phone calls and she's not goin' anywhere 'til this baby gets here."

"And you know what?" He began. "I'm stayin' out of her way because I have enough to deal with right now and I'm not

lettin' her complicate things any more than they already are."
"Enough is enough."

"It might seem that way but one thing that'll help get you through is to make yourself give God thanks for your trouble." He continued. "And I know that sounds totally against common sense but that's what it takes for peace of mind and that goes a long way, believe me when I tell you."

"This has to be God because I was just readin' that the other day and I remember thinkin', how can you be thankful for your trouble?"

"I think you know because this isn't the first time you've been through a little trouble and whatever you've been through has made you stronger."

"It doesn't really feel like it but if you say so." He said as he managed to laugh a little.

"You're probably bein' too hard on yourself but other people can see how well you're handlin' things." He told him. "You're about to do somethin' that most guys wouldn't and you won't regret it as long as you keep the Lord head of your house." "Do what Paul says to do in that fifth chapter of Ephesians and watch what the Lord will do in your marriage." "He'll bless you for your obedience and she will too, believe me when I tell you."

"That simple huh?"

"It's simple and hard at the same time because it takes work to make it what God intended it to be." "And to get back to what happened today, she's watchin' you and your reaction to this whole picture and what she sees from you is gonna be an indicator of what kind of husband you'll be."

"We were walkin' through the house about an hour before it happened and she was tellin' me that she couldn't believe that all of this was happenin' for her." Michael said then. "She said that it was too good to be true and then this happened and threw everything off." He said, shaking his head. "We were sittin' at a red light and then pow, it was like we were in another world for a second."

"And out came Jesus, I already know man, I've been there."

"You already know and I said to myself, my babies, this can't be happenin.'" He continued. "And I was tryin' to stay calm because I didn't want her to panic but evidently it was enough to send her into labor." "I talked to her a half hour ago and they told her that she won't be goin' home tonight so there it is."

"And don't start blamin' yourself, she was just a couple of weeks from goin' anyway, so man up and keep it movin' because believe me, she's takin' notes." "She's had some negative experiences with men and this is your chance to let God help you step up and do what He made us to do."

"I don't have a problem with that but it's a little hard when you're not together yet, you know what I mean?"

"But that day's comin' and what you shouldn't do is put a lot of pressure on her because what she's about to go through is a major life change." "I've seen it five separate times and it's mental and physical too and because she's so young, you may see and hear some things comin' from her that you don't expect so don't take anything personal, it's part of the process."

"Then thanks for the warnin' because any kind of heads up with this is gonna help me." He began. "I'm startin' to feel like this is my fault and I know exactly where that's comin' from."

"Then since you know, use the power God gave you to rebuke that thought and keep it movin.'" "Any device that your enemy will use to try to take your peace of mind belongs you know where, so take the upper hand and do what you have to do."

"And that's stuff that I already knew but it helps to hear it from somebody else." Michael said as he started back out of the lot.

"This can be a good experience for you because there's gonna be some other stuff comin' but just know that God is faithful."

"We were just about to contact you, your husband went into a cardiac arrest event about an hour ago and we have him downstairs in I.C.U. again." Marie was told after going up to the C.C.U. to see Jerry.

"You are kiddin' me." She responded then in shock.

"We don't want you to worry, we have him stabilized down there and we're waiting on his doctor to order a heart scan to see what the problem is." The practitioner told her.

She nodded as she found a nearby seat after having a brief dizzy spell.

"Is there anyone else here with you?"

"My sister is upstairs in labor and my mother is here with her so maybe I just need to go back up there and you can text me when you know somethin'."

"We don't want you to worry, they're watching him really closely and we'll keep in contact with you."

"I called Donna and let her know what happened and she said Randy would probably be here after dinner." Marie remarked with Kathryn in the waiting area ten minutes later. "And I didn't ask him to be here but it really does help."

"You didn't think he'd be anywhere else did you?"

"I can't expect everybody to drop what they're doin' just because of my problems, how unfair is that?"

"I wouldn't call it unfair, it's just what family does and one thing that I've found out since I moved here is that this is a tight one." Kathryn continued as she handed her a tissue before putting an arm around her. "And I've never told anybody else this but when everybody found out about how Janice got here, I was expectin' a lot of hateful phone calls and this and that because of what happened." "Then when I got the reaction from Frances that I did, that's when God started to deal with me by showin' me how much more I needed than what I had."

Marie nodded then, determined not to lose control of her emotions.

"And I'm sayin' all of that to help you to see that God allows different things to happen to all of us to get us where He wants us to be." "Jerry's gonna be okay and I'm sayin' that by faith but what you have to do is relax and put all of this in God's hands and stop relyin' on yourself." "Let this family be involved because believe me when I tell you, the Lord is with 'em and they know how to get in touch with Him."

"I know you're right but it's not lookin' good mother and my mind is goin' too far ahead and makin' me worry about this whole situation."

"But we're doin' everything we can and He's in God's hands, don't you ever forget that." "And right now, you need to be thinkin' about his baby that you're carryin' because you don't want your stress to make things worse do you?"

She shook her head, agreeing with her.

"Then what we're gonna do is concentrate on believin' God and I'm gonna tell you somethin' that Florence told me the other day." Kathryn said, pausing. "When she was goin' through that thing with her lung cancer, she said Douglas told her that the worse a situation is, the more glory God will get after He does the work."

"Typical Douglas." Marie said as she managed to laugh a little.

"And you know it." "And when him and Frances get together, you can almost count on a positive outcome." Kathryn said.

"And they were here that first night because they know that prayer works." She said as they noticed Mary Ann coming towards them then.

"You must be talkin' about me, is that why you stopped?" She asked them.

"No we weren't." Marie told her, determined not to escalate the conversation. "How's she doin'?"

"They want her to get up and start walkin' but she doesn't want to be by herself." She answered a moment later. "I told her I'd walk with her but she wants one of you to be with her but where is what's his face, what's his name?" She asked, referring to Michael. "He's the reason why she's here ahead of time, so where is he?" She insisted.

"Okay, we need to get this straight." Marie responded then. "Number one, the accident that they were in was not his fault, somebody hit them from behind." She said, coming to his defense.

"Were you there, how do you know that for a fact?"

"Wait a minute, I'm not finished." Marie added with a calm tone. "And you're not gonna see him up here for reasons that you probably wouldn't understand so I'm not gonna waste my time tryin' to explain it to you."

"Then if he's so much in love with her and he says that he's gonna take care of this baby, where is he?" "Why isn't he gonna be here when she's born, can you tell me that much?" "He needs to be in there holdin' her hand or walkin' with her or somethin, and you know I'm right." She concluded with air of disgust, mixed with building anger and frustration.

"No you're not ma'am and I don't think this is the time or the place for us to be goin' back and forth about it." Marie told her as she stood up and started towards Janice's room.

"You might be walkin' away from me but I'm not goin' anywhere." "This baby is just as much a part of me as you are so get used to it."

"You don't know how close I came to lookin' at her and tellin' the devil to back off because that's exactly what all of that was, I could almost feel it." Marie remarked fifteen minutes later as she and Janice slowly walked the halls, waiting for regular contractions to begin.

"And she asked me the same thing, she wanted to know why he wasn't up here with me and I just couldn't make her understand why that couldn't happen." She said as she braced for another contraction that "stopped her in her tracks."

"Honey don't tense up, I heard that that makes it worse." Marie told her as she put an arm around her waist.

"I'm tryin' not to but this is worse than I thought it would be." She said, trying to keep her composure. She said a minute later. "And I told one of the nurses not to let her back in there because she's makin' me almost wanna smack her face but I'm not goin' there." She confessed."She's not gonna take me back where I used to be but she just needs to stay out of the way right now."

"Are you stayin' in touch with Michael?"

She nodded. "Douglas took him to get a rental car and he went on back to his house, he said that he needed to be by himself." Janice said as she held her back. "He said that him and the Lord needed to have a talk because nobody else understands how he feels right now." She managed to say.

"Sometimes you have to do that and by this time tomorrow, things are gonna look a whole lot better." She said with a spirit of faith and confidence.

"I don't quite know what it is but I'm havin' a hard time stayin' away from here." Randy remarked half an hour later back downstairs with Marie.

"And you know what?" She began. "You have no clue how much I appreciate what you did and what you're doin' to help Jerry because I'm too close to this situation to be much good." She admitted.

"But what else can you do, you're here for him and he might not realize it but you're here and that means a lot." He emphasized.

"I'm not really too sure about that because it doesn't matter what I say or do, it's never enough for him." "It's like he's in his own world and won't listen to people that are tryin' to help him."

"He may be listenin' more than you think he is, you can't always go by what you see." "And sometimes it's a guy thing, we don't always like to pay attention to women because it bruises the ego, you know what I mean?"

"Yeah I've heard that before but right now, he's not ready to make right decisions." "One of the nurses told me that he said he's been thinkin' about just walkin' ouf of here and flyin' back home because he's tired of bein' on his back."

"And this was before this happened today?"

"It was a couple of days ago, maybe Wednesday or Thursday." "And now they wanna say that he's clinically depressed and it's just too much right now, so what I've decided to do is just give it up to God because it's too big for me." She said as she noticed a text message from Michael.

"Everything alright?" Randy asked her a few moments later.

She nodded. "Michael's just checkin' up on Janice, he said he's havin' trouble tryin' to sleep and he has to work tonight."

"I can tell that they're really in to each other so this has got be hard on him but what do you do but keep him encouraged."

"She's makin' some progress and I'm goin' back up there in a few minutes but all he can do is wait it out."

"Sweetheart we're going to break your water and get an epidural into you and you'll feel a lot better, we promise." Janice's nurse told her an hour later after checking her progress.

She managed to nod a little through her tears brought on by repeated painful contractions and the sudden flashback of the night that

Craig had forced himself on her, resulting in these moments of nearly unbearable pangs of childbirth.

"You're almost halfway there so you're making good progress." She was told by the nurse a few moments later. "I'm calling the anesthesiologist and we're gonna make you feel a whole lot better." "And if you keep going like this, she'll be here by nine or ten, how does that sound?" She asked her.

"Really?" "I thought it would be twelve hours or more." She managed to say as she recovered from her last contraction.

"That's usually the way it goes but your accident may have had something to do with you going so quickly." She added as she read her graph. "So keep up the good work hon, you're getting there fast and furious."

"That must be some strong stuff because you've been out for a couple of hours." Marie remarked around eight-thirty after Janice suddenly woke up.

"I can't feel my legs." She said, alarmed.

"You're not supposed to, you're numb from your waist down and that's why you're not feelin' the pains you're having." Marie told her. "I'm takin' notes in my head because I'm gonna be doin' this too."

"This is crazy." Janice began then. "They had me sittin' on the side of the bed and they put this needle in my back and it started workin' almost right away." She continued, puzzled by the experience. "And then I remember layin' here thinkin' about how this happened and all I could hear in my head was "forgive him." She finished as tears began to flow down her face as the attending nurse came in the room to check on her progress.

Honey you had a good nap didn't you?" She asked her before Marie stepped back out of the room.

"I didn't think you could sleep when you're in labor." Janice admitted then.

"When your epidural works like it should, you can." She said as she slipped on exam gloves. "And by the looks of your contractions, they've been coming every five minutes." She added as she glanced at the paper graph. "Let's see where you are, relax for me." She said as she experienced another that caused her to cry out in a different kind of pain.

"Oh my God, you're having this baby now." She said a few moments later after checking her. "I need you to push if you can with the next contraction." She added as she slipped on a surgical gown. "You're gonna see your baby within the next five minutes.

"I went down the hall to get somethin' out of the vendin' machine and when I got back, the door was shut and I thought somethin' had gone wrong in here." Marie remarked an hour later with Janice and Kathryn as they watched a nurse give Kristen her first bath.

"Sometimes it happens that way but she really came quick for a first baby."

"Does Mary Ann know that she's here?" Janice asked Marie then.

"I sent her a text and she said she's on her way." "She didn't say where she was and I didn't ask either." She said, shaking her head a little.

"I sent Michael a picture of her and he sent me back a cryin' emoji." Janice said as she watched every move of her newborn child, conceived from a violent, selfish act but nevertheless a life, given to her by God to train up to know Him. As her mind went back to the night that Douglas had boldly informed her that disposing of it was "not an option," she became overwhelmed with gratitude at the circumstances that lead her to family that love and respect life.

"What's her weight?" Kathryn enquired of the nurse as she began to wash her hair under the faucet.

"She weighed in at exactly six pounds and that's pretty good because she was a couple of weeks early." "She's a little doll."

"I'll be back." Marie said then after receiving a text from the cardiac care unit to come downstairs to speak with Jerry's physician. "Love you, you did good." She added as she hugged Janice before leaving the room.

"We noticed on the scan that we did an hour ago that one of the stents that were implanted into his heart somehow shifted, and caused a blood clot to form." Jerry's doctor informed Marie ten minutes later. "And I don't mind saying it because I've seen this happen before." He continued. "Somebody somewhere had to be praying for him because he was on the verge of another attack so evidently, it wasn't his time to go."

She nodded then as she tried to contain herself, while inwardly rejoicing at the power of prayer.

"What we don't want to do is take him back to surgery so soon after his procedure last week so we've given him an intravenous blood thinner that will dissovle the clotting." He continued as he showed her a rough drawing of what was occuring. "We're going to keep him here in the I.C.U. for another twenty four hours to make sure that he can go back on the C.C.U."

"So if everything starts to look like it should, how soon can we get him out of here?" Marie asked him then.

"When we see that his heart is working like it should after looking at E.K.G.s, it may be another week." "And I know that sounds like an eternity but we don't want the same thing to happen all over again because he wouldn't survive another attack."

"A week goes fast but he's not the type to stay on his back like this."

"We understand that and we'll do everything we can to get him up and out and recovered." "And we know that you just found out that you're expecting your first baby, so congratulations and that's another incentive for him to get well."

She nodded then in agreement with him.

"So that means that you can't be stressing yourself out over this because you have to take care of yourself too." He told her with genuine concern. "You're not here alone are you?"

"No I'm not, my sister just had a baby up there a couple of hours ago so I've been goin' back and forth between here and there." She said as she slowly stood up.

"I know that's exciting but you look a little tired so I recommend that you go home and get some rest and things will look a lot better tomorrow, I promise you."

"Oh my God, give her to me." Mary Ann remarked as she walked into Janice's room half an hour later.

She nodded reluctantly as she approched her bed to take hold of her one and only grandchild and it was then that Mary Ann broke into a heartfelt wail of a mother who had lost her son. This connection to him in the form of his baby caused a bittersweet reaction from her that ultimately began to have an effect on Janice as she allowed herself to feel a sense of compassion for her that had been absent before this moment.

"My sweetheart, you're all that I have." Mary Ann sobbed as she sat down in a nearby chair with Kristen in her arms. "I'm your grandmother and your father would've loved you more than anybody else and when you're old enough to understand, I'm going to make sure that you know all about him." She continued as she held her close to her I'm going to make sure that he doesn't mistreat you or cause you any problems because if he does, he's in big trouble with me." She concluded as she began to slowly rock back and forth with her when Kathryn walked in with Florence then.

"Oh my Lord, what a little doll." Florence remarked as she approached the chair where Mary Ann was sitting to get a quick look.

"What are you doing here, you are not a part of this baby's family." Mary Ann demanded of her through more falling tears.

It was then that Janice reached over to the call button to summon her nurse to the room.

"I don't want you anywhere near this baby because I don't trust you." She continued then.

"Is everything ok?" The floor nurse asked as she appeared a minute later.

"Can you take her down to the nursery for right now?" Janice asked, fighting her overflowing emotions.

"Is there a problem here?" She asked as she approached Mary Ann.

"No there's not a problem, I'm this baby's grandmother and I have a right to protect her." She insisted.

"Ma'am there's nothing going on here that's hurting her but her mom wants us to take her down to the nursery for a while." She said as she reached for Kristen. "And if that's going to be a problem for you I can get security in here, okay?" She asked her with quiet and firm professionalism.

"When will I be able to see her again?" Mary Ann persisted. "I live in Washington D.C. and I have to get back there by tomorrow." She said as she reluctantly let her go.

"Ma'am that's really up to the baby's mother but right now, you need to calm down and stop causing trouble in here." She replied as she abruptly stood up and came at Janice as if she had done her harm.

"Why should I calm down?" She asked, while keeping her eyes directly on Janice. "A white man killed my son and your baby's father and I don't want her close to any of 'em, do you understand me girl?" "You need to move out of that house that you're livin' in because I don't want her there." She finally finished as she turned to walk out of the room before flipping two fingers at Florence.

"Oh my, did I do something wrong?" Florence asked then, somewhat confused.

"You didn't do anything, she's the one that's havin' the problem right now." Kathryn said as she walked over to Janice who was having a normal, post partum meltdown. "And what you have to do is remember where all of that came from." She continued as she pulled a blanket over her and handed her a tissue. "We all know that and all of us remember what we were like before the Lord saved us." She emphasized.

Janice nodded then in agreement with her.

"But what you need to do now is try to get some sleep because you've had some kind of a day and it's nothin' but God that everybody is okay." She added as she took her hands into hers. "You're a mother now so you have to take care of yourself so you can do what you have to do for your baby."

"Have they told you when you're coming home dear?" Florence asked her.

"Tuesday or Wednesday and I'm worried about Michael." She admitted. "He called off from work tonight and that's not like him to do that."

"Marie talked to him and they told him that he has the time so it's not a problem so stop worryin', close your eyes and get some rest." Kathryn said as she motioned for Florence to follow her out. "I'll call you in the mornin.'"

"Man I wouldn't have been much good if I had gone to work tonight, I wasn't gonna fake it because too much is goin' on in my head." Michael remarked with James and Frances out on the deck around ten 'o clock.

"Settle yourself down son, it's all okay." Frances told him. "This starts a whole new chapter for you and I know it's all gonna work out and if I were you, I'd start thankin' God in advance for what's comin'." She added with faith and confidence.

"I don't think anybody realizes how much hearin' things like that are helpin' me to get over, I'm not kiddin'."

"And you have to go through things before you have testimonies that won't ever leave you." James told him. "This whole thing with Janice and how you've let the Lord keep you on the right track is gonna work out to your advantage." "You don't do the right thing and God not back you up, and it doesn't really matter what it looks like either."

"And the right thing is to thank God for what you're goin' through and I know that sounds a bit strange but I also know that it works in your favor." Frances told him.

"And you know what, I'm gettin' there, believe it or not." Michael said, shaking his head.

"I know that you are and the first time I heard about that scripture was right after I was left with four kids to raise by myself." She began. "William took off and God stepped in and it didn't matter that I was havin' my little pity parties and wonderin' why the Lord would let this happen to me." "It was time for me to grow up so by the time your big brother Douglas showed up at my door and blew smoke in my face, I knew how to get in touch with God."

"And I asked him one time about why he did that." Michael said, laughing with her.

"What was his answer?" James asked.

"He said that he was puttin' you to the test to see how real you were." He began. "Irene had told him some stuff about how she grew up goin' to church two or three times a week etc, etc, and he was tryin' to see exactly how churchy you were."

"But what he didn't understand was that it wasn't those four walls that was givin' me what I needed to make it." "He didn't know that he was up against the power of God's spirit and that's what you've got to do." She continued. "The Lord didn't give you the Holy Ghost for you to fail your test and these situations that you're dealin' with like Miss Mary Ann and what happened this afternoon with the accident and all of the stuff that comes with it, is workin' together for your good."

"And that's what keepin' me awake, I already know I'm not sleepin' tonight, forget that."

"Are you worried about Janice?" James asked him.

"Worry isn't quite the word but the accident was kind of a wake up call." He said after a moment. "I know that her and Kristen are okay, thank the Lord, but the question in my mind is what are we waitin' on?"

"Are you worried about the house not quite done yet?"

"That's part of it." "I'm not about to move her and a new baby in there like it is." "I'm there, but with them, it's a whole different picture and I can't do it." He finished, shaking his head.

"If we really concentrate on it, we could probably have it done in a month to six weeks from now." James said. "Would that work out for you?"

"When she and Kristen get here in a couple of days, I'm gonna sit down with her and see what she thinks about that." He said after a moment. "If we can get everything done by the first of November, then maybe by Thanksgiving, it'll all be a done deal."

"So break it down for me honey." Frances told him then as he suddenly reacted to a picture of Kristen that suddenly appeared on his phone with a text message from Marie. Then without saying a word, he passed it over to her before he slowly stood up and went into the house to be by himself with his emotions. He began to feel a confirmation in his spirit that this was "meant to be" and there was no longer a shred of doubt about his unconventional decision to raise another man's child as his own. He began to feel inexplicably freed of the burden he had been carrying the majority of the day because of the accident and willfully "gave it to God" whose yoke is easy and burdens are light.

As he began to walk through the darkened house, from room to room he allowed the Lord to lift his burdens from the day and move forward, now knowing that he was in the will of God.

Chapter 4

September 15
Tuesday

"I can't really explain it but I took one look at this picture and that was it." Michael remarked Tuesday evening at the table with Irene and Douglas after dinner. "There were things goin' on in my mind that I didn't like then all of a sudden, Marie sent me this and somethin' happened."

"Was it like one of those moments when you feel like the Lord hit you with a lightnin' bolt?" Irene asked him as they laughed together.

"Have you ever felt really heavy and burdened about somethin' and then the Lord comes by and just takes it?" He asked her after a moment.

"And you know it and you can't really explain it til it happens to you so I know where you're comin' from."

"I heard from my insurance company yesterday and I found out that I had gap coverage on the car so they're gonna pay off the last two payments I had on it." He began. "But I've got to find another car without gettin' into a lot of debt so it is what it is, I refuse to complain about it because it could've been a lot worse."

"This baby looks like her mother, how does that grab you?" Douglas asked him as he passed his phone back to him.

"I think that's a good thing because she's the prettiest girl in the world." He said without hesitation. "And she was worried because of the sonogram she had that looked just like him." He said, referring to Craig.

"And you can't always go by that because they change so much and when you actually see her, it might really hit you." Irene told him.

"I know it will but somethin' happened to me Sunday night that I just can't explain right now." He emphasized again.

"So what's the plan you have in mind?" Douglas asked him.

"After she comes home and gets settled in, I think we need to sit down together and decide on a date." He began. "I'm workin' with James to see if we can have the house ready in about six weeks because I refuse to bring her and Kristen in there until it's really ready." He added with a sober tone about him.

"What's left to do in there, I can't wait to see it." Irene commented.

"She showed me the laminate that she wants because we pulled up all of the carpet." He began as he scrolled through the pictures on his phone to show her. "The wall is gone between the livingroom and dining room so it'll be one big space." He said as Terry and Sheila came up the steps.

"There you are, I've been tryin' to get in touch with you." Sheila told Michael as she sat down.

"I sort of kind of turned my phone off for a minute, I was givin' myself a chance to organize my mind." He said. "And I told Janice that too so we can just decompress, you know what I mean?"

"Yeah I get it, the last couple of days have been stressful, I already know." "After my accident, all I could do was a lot of prayin' and lettin' God help me because it just threw everything off, you know what I mean?"

"I do now and I keep tellin' myself that it could've been so much worse because it was probably five minutes before it happened that I reminded her to put her seat belt on." Michael said, shaking his head.

"Because the Lord knew what was about to happen." Sheila said. "And He's good like that."

"He hit us so hard that the back of this phone flew off and I was surprised that it still worked after I got it back together."

"So was he just not payin' attention or what?" Terry asked him.

"After it happened, he got out of his car and said man I'm sorry, I was textin' my girl and I wasn't lookin' where I was goin'." He said imitating him. "And it wasn't nothin' but my Holy Ghost that kept me from makin' a scene out there, I'm serious."

"But you didn't and that's what counts."

"And no insurance huh?" Sheila asked him.

"None, nada, zilch, however you wanna say it." "I heard him tellin' the police that he lost his job and couldn't pay his bills so he's got some problems."

"So they're comin' home tomorrow?"

He nodded. "Marie and her mother are takin' care of that and it'll be a couple of days before I show up over there." "She needs some time to get settled."

"So what's goin' on with Jerry, is he out of the I.C.U.?" Irene asked her.

"She told me that he woke up Monday mornin' and he wouldn't talk to her." Sheila said. "She hasn't called anybody else because she doesn't want us to worry."

"But she can't go through this by herself, why is she thinkin' like that?"

"She said this is between her and Jerry and she doesn't think he'd want her talkin' about it to anybody else." "So I told her we're all prayin',that's about all she wants right now."

"And that can do more than all of us combined so just keep at it." Douglas remarked.

"Are you ready for my stuff?" Sheila asked him as she opened her laptop case.

"If you're ready for me to see it." "How much more do you have?"

"I've got fifty pages and I'm tryin' to get at least seventy five so Irene, it's your turn ma'am."

"I figured I'd be next."

"Of course you are because if you hadn't done what you did, we might not be sittin' here talkin' about what the Lord did for your wonderful husband." Sheila said, waiting on his reaction.

"Wonderful?" He asked, disagreeing with her. "That's a word fit for the Lord by himself, don't go there."

"But you know what I mean because we all know how God uses you to help people out of their messes, bottom line." She added as she handed him the printed pages for his examination. "And if you see anything in there that you want changed, let me know and I won't be offended, I promise."

"It's really good Douglas and I found out some stuff that I didn't know about you." Terry said as she sat down with a plate. "And after it's published, I'm buyin' some copies and givin' 'em out to people that I think will actually take the time to read it."

"How long are you givin' me to read through this ma'am?" He asked Sheila after a moment.

"There's no rush because I want you to be really satisfied with it." She began. "So if you see somethin' in there that doesn't seem right, this is the time to let me know so I can add or take away, you know what I mean?"

"Have you found somebody to publish it yet?" Irene asked her.

"Yes ma'am, I've done my homework on that and this is gonna make a difference to somebody out there that needs to know that there's help from God if they want it."

"And that's the whole thing, if you don't know that you need help, it's a lost cause until the Lord starts to deal with you." Douglas remarked as he skimmed through the contents of the manuscript.

"And that's what happened with Aunt Kathryn." "We didn't know that she was in there listenin' to what you were talkin' about and she must've heard somethin' that struck a nerve."

"Have you interviewed her or asked her what it was?" Irene asked .

"Not yet and after I get your story on paper, her and Aunt Frances are next."

"I think you're serious."

"As a heart attack as they say". "And I don't think I'll make a lot of money from this but that's not the point."

"So what do you want from me?" Irene asked her.

"I remember talkin' to Aunt Frances one day about the day you called her." She started, recalling the day soon after Janice moved from D.C.

"I'll never forget it, I felt like I was ten years old callin' my mama but I didn't know what else to do."

"And Douglas if any of this is makin' you uncomfortable, let me know sir." Sheila told him as she typed on her laptop.

"It's not about me and if you say that the Lord has lead you to do this, who am I to let my pride get in the way?" "It is what it is and I hate to think of where'd I'd be if she hadn't called mama."

"Do you remember what you said to her?" Terry asked her.

"Like it was yesterday." "I got on the phone and I was cryin' so hard that she thought somebody had died or got hurt or somethin.'" She recalled. "All I could say was I don't know what to do, I don't know what to do, then she asked me, what's wrong with Douglas?"

"She just knew didn't she?" Michael asked her.

"She didn't know what was goin' on but she knew that somethin' was up." "I told her what happened with Phil and that he couldn't eat or sleep because of what he saw and that he was talkin' about killin' himself."

"It was like a video playin' over and over again in my mind and that was the only way I thought I could stop it." Douglas injected. "And when you're in that state of mind, that's when the devil really moves in to take you out and if it wasn't for her tellin' me what I needed to do, I wouldn't be here now." He said with a knowing tone.

"She told me to put him on the phone and back then, you could listen in on the extension and I heard her say that you need to come to church and let God help you." Irene continued. "And we all know that you don't have to be in a church building before the Lord will help you but she told me later that's what the Lord told her to tell him."

"And I thought to myself, are you kiddin' me?" Douglas said then. " I came really close to actually sayin' what I was thinkin' but before I knew it, I told her yeah okay and hung up on her." "That's how foul and evil that spirit was in me and I knew good and well what I had planned so it didn't matter what she thought about me."

"I don't think you told us that part before did you?" Sheila asked him. "And Irene, I'm not done with you yet, just sit tight over there." She told her as she continued to type.

"I had put a silencer on Brutus and the plan was to go out to the car and just end it, blow my brains out because it had gotten to the place where it was unbearable." "I tried sleepin' pills, crack, weed, booze, you name it and nothin' would work."

"And I would've gotten up in the mornin' and gone outside and seen a mess and it wasn't nothin' but God that changed the whole scenario." Irene spoke up then.

"So what actually stopped you from goin' out there with Brutus?" Sheila asked, trying not to laugh at the pistol's name.

"You tell me." "I don't have any answer to that except the Lord was answerin' a lot of prayers from the woman that I had hung up on." He said, shaking his head at the thought. "I can remember sittin' in the dark about midnight with a crack pipe and the next thing I knew the sun was comin' up."

"And I went in the livingroom and asked him if he was goin' to church like he said he would." Irene said. "And I hardly ever went myself but I thought it might help a little so I pressed the issue."

"You had no idea did you?" Michael asked her.

"I really didn't." "I had in my mind that he might let somebody pray for him and that would be the end of it but I should've known better." "I was a big time pew baby and I had seen a lot of things happen but me and my stubborn self didn't let it phase me after a while, all of the stuff that I saw happen was for other people, not me." She admitted.

"You were numb in other words." Sheila said.

"Exactly, that's a good word for it, so you know how shocked I was when I saw God do what He does." "I look up from whatever I was doin' and see this man get up and walk down to the altar and I'm seriously trippin.'" "I couldn't believe what I was seein', it was a little surreal actually."

"It was surreal to me too but you've heard enough from me, you came to get another perspective." Douglas said as he continued to read through her work. "And besides that, you know the end of the story and I don't need to be repetitive, you know what I mean?"

"We know the story because we're your family but this needs to be out there for people to know that there's hope in God." Sheila insisted. "And I see where you're comin' from but you have an experience that most people don't and things are gettin' worse and worse so how do you hold back?"

"You know me better than that but it's one thing to tell people how to come out of the wilderness and another for that to actually happen." He answered. "I had to be knocked up side my head to come to myself and at some point in here, you might wanna stress the point about not waitin' until tomorrow when you feel the Lord dealin' with you."

"Because you might not see tomorrow huh?"

"You got it." "And a lot of times I still wonder why it was him instead of me that died that day." "I was just as high as he was but because of my mother-in law's prayers, I was spared."

"She was callin' my name out too so what was my problem?" Irene asked, laughing a little.

"Honey you're the only one that can answer that." Douglas told her. "And to this day, I wish I had known about this all of my life like you have because I think I would've saved myself and a lot of other people some grief."

"But it's good that you're willin' to help me put this out there." Sheila began. "I mean everybody wouldn't be and it's not that you're dwellin' on the past but you're rememberin' and givin' God the glory for how He's makin' a new creature out of you."

"You preachin'?" Michael asked her.

"Not at all but this is somethin' that I can't get away from." She continued. "Your testimony reminds me of the Red Sea and the road to Damascus all put together and God doesn't want Israel to forget how they were delivered out of Egypt and that was thousands of years ago."

"You're absolutely right, I can't argue with you."

"But I see your point too." "You're not that comfortable talkin' about yourself but sometimes we have to get out of our comfort zones to help somebody and I know you know that but I'm just puttin' my two cents in there, you know what I mean?"

"Your two cents are worth somethin' because you're the author of this." Irene told her.

"This is just somethin' that the Lord put on my heart to do and I know when that happens, it has to be for a good reason." Sheila said then. "And you might really be surprised at how many couples break up because of things like what you went through."

"Do you have any idea how close we came to bustin' up'?" Irene asked her. "And it would've been my fault because of my stubborn thinkin' and I should've known better, but me and my selfishness couldn't think of anybody but myself and how my life was gonna change."

"So you're sayin' that you were on your way out the door because of how different things were gonna be because he got himself together."

"That's pretty much it and even though I knew deep in my gut that he had done the right thing, I wasn't goin' for it." She admitted "I was too busy feelin' sorry for my stupid self because we weren't gonna be out doin' stuff that I knew we didn't have any business doin' and I think I was tryin' to prove a point to anybody that knew how I grew up."

"Can I quote you on that?" Sheila asked her as she continued typing.

"Honey this is your book, you're the author and if you think that might make a difference in some kind of way, I'm not gettin' in your way." She told her. "Pride doesn't get you anywhere and if I would hold some stuff back just because things were makin' me look bad, what kind of witness is that?" "I was a hot mess and it really was too bad that Paul had to come and get in my face before the light bulb in my head finally came on."

"Wow." Sheila remarked. "Can you remember anything that he said?"

"He said a lot of things and you know how Paul does not bite his tongue." She said after a moment. "And I think when he told me that I should've been followin' my husband down to the altar instead of standin' in his way, that struck a nerve with me and I started gettin' myself together." She added, shaking her head.

"So what were you doin' that made him go there with you?" Michael asked her. "And if you don't wanna answer that, I understand but since we're talkin' about it, you might as well come out with it."

"And I love you too Michael Johnson." She responded with a laugh. "And Paul might not even remember doin' this but somehow he found out that I had done somethin' off, tryin' to see how serious he was about startin' all over again." She continued. "I went out and bought a couple of pints of Hennessy and sat 'em on the counter top one night, just to see what would happen." "It was our anniversary and I was testin' him out, big time." She admitted again.

"I got up the next mornin' and saw these two bottles standin' side by side and it was almost like two eyes lookin' right at me, and I kid you not." Douglas said, laughing again. " I knew exactly what was goin' on and it made me even more determined not to go there anymore." "I was done but what that did had a lot to do with the relationship that I have with your Aunt Frances."

"Which is priceless, I already know." Sheila said.

"It is and the reason I say that is because of the way she knew what I needed to hear when, does that make sense?"

"It makes a lot of sense and you know when that happens, it has to be the Lord takin' care of you."

"Absolutely." "It was a couple of days after that happened that she called me at work and told me to stop by her house because she needed to talk to me."

"Was that the first time she did that?"

"It was but I went on my lunch hour and she opened the door and took me by my hand and almost made me sit down next to her."

"Did that scare you?" Terry asked him.

"Scared wasn't the word but I thought I might've done somethin' wrong and she was about to take me to the woodshed but that couldn't have been any farther from the truth." He said as he recalled the details of the day. "She sat me down in that breakfast nook and looked me straight in the eye and said the Lord told me to tell you that He's fightin' your battles and to stay strong." He continued. "And that's not news to us now but at the time, it was what I needed to hear." "I was about a month and a half old and she knew that you don't leave new babies to themselves without nourishment and that's how we started to click."

"You have a chemistry that's unbelievable and that's pretty unusual." Sheila remarked.

"I wouldn't take a million dollars for what I've been able to learn from her." "And it's one thing to get it at church from bible classes or whatever but there's nothin' like havin' that one on one instruction, especially when you don't have any idea what holiness means." "I was fresh out of the world and she understood that but that's what love does, it gives and that's what she made up her mind to do."

"And this was when I really wasn't talkin' to her." Irene put in. "I was mad because I thought she was partly responsible for what happened and when I think about that now, how could I have been so off in my head?"

"You mean just because she asked him to come to church the next day, you stopped talkin' to your mama?" Sheila asked her, surprised.

"You heard me right and I think that's what made Paul come to my house and let me have it."

"He does not play, I was at their house one day a couple of weeks ago, and he runs that place and those kids like a man on a mission." Michael commented. "They're crazy about their daddy but he doesn't take any off behavior from 'em either."

"Because they're doin' what they're supposed to by trainin' 'em up in the way they're supposed to go, and if we had had half of what they're bein' taught, Junkyard might not've existed but that's another story and I won't go there." Douglas said.

"But Junkyard did exist and that's what this is all about." Sheila told him. "This is about how the blood of Jesus took all of that away and started you all over again and that goes for all of us in here, but there was somethin' more dramatic about your experience, you know what I mean?"

"It was that, I agree with you but I've already had my say, this is about my other half sittin' over there." He said referring to Irene.

"Can I ask you a question that I just happened to think about?" Michael asked her.

"Go for it."

"What did you do with those two pints?" He asked, trying to keep a straight face.

"I gave 'em to a couple of girlfriends that we used to run around with and they didn't believe me when I told 'em that my little test didn't work." She answered after a moment. "And I seriously thought that I had it hands down but I should've known better." "I knew deep down in my gut that he had done the right thing but stubborness and pride are two dangerous things and I was full of both of 'em."

"But why weren't you glad about it ma'am?" Sheila asked her. "I have an idea what your answer's gonna be but I have to hear it from you before I put it on paper."

"I was havin' too good of a time doin' stuff and goin' places that I didn't do growin' up and I knew that he wasn't gonna be runnin' with me anymore and I seriously resented it." She admitted. "I even tried to do stuff out there on my own and fell flat on my face and that made it even worse."

"So what was the reaction of everybody once they found out about Junkyard goin' to the church house?"

"Shock is probably the best word and I heard stuff like a phase that wasn't gonna last and it was just a matter of time before he'd be back." Irene said. "Everybody knew what happened to Phillip and it was a thing like when you get over it, we'll have our Junkyard back."

"You were actually hearin' stuff like that?" Sheila asked her.

"I was and I was probably thinkin' the same things but just not sayin' 'em out loud and that's how much help I needed but just didn't know it." "I was caught up in my feelings and what my life was gonna be like." She finished, shaking her head at the thought.

"This is gonna be a good book and I can't wait to read it once it's all put together." Terry remarked. "I don't know who it'll end up helpin' but this is a good thing you're doin' and I can't wait to hear what Aunt Frances has to say." "Her stuff brings water to my eyes."

"Why do you think she's my best friend?" Michael asked her.

"I had her first, so there." Douglas said, laughing along with them."

"I really had her first but I didn't realize what I had until stuff started to happen." Irene remarked. "And what that taught me was to never take anything or anybody for granted because you never know how much you miss somebody until the communication breaks down."

"So who was the one that started talkin' again?"

"After Paul told me about myself, I got up the nerve to call and apologize for my attitude and it was like nothin' had ever happened." She began. "Then she went on to tell me that I had a new husband that I needed to support instead of workin' against him because it wasn't gonna work."

"How come I've never known about that conversation?" Douglas asked her.

"I don't really have an answer for that but it made me think." "Between what her and Paul said to me, I pretty much gave it up and let God help me." She said. "And it hurt my pride at first but when I really started to get out of my feelin's and got serious about wantin' the Holy Ghost, that's when things started to get better."

"No more dirty little tricks huh?" Michael asked her.

"None." "I was finally startin' to realize that I wasn't gettin' anywhere and I was wastin' my time tryin' to undo what God had done." She said as her text notification sounded. "I had no clue that the devil was usin' me and that's how far I had gotten." She concluded before reading the message from Marie.

"What's the matter, you look like somethin's up." Sheila asked her half a minute later.

"Everybody please pray, the hospital just called a minute ago and told me that Jerry just checked himself out." "Trying to call him but no answer." "I'll get back with you." Irene read then.

"You are kiddin'." Sheila remarked then after a short moment.

"He's strong enough to do that?" Terry asked, surprised

by what they had just heard.

"He might feel like he is but you don't get over open heart surgery this quick and she's probably in panic mode right about now."

"Anybody that feels like we can change this, meet me downstairs in five minutes." Douglas said then as he started to stand up.

"I think he means business." Sheila said, as they followed his lead.

"I know that we all could've gone somewhere by ourselves and got some prayers through but that's not how I feel led about this." Douglas remarked five minutes later after the four of them had come together in his basement office. "This is an emergency but God knows exactly where Jerry is and He knows how to protect him and get him back here if that's what needs to happen."

"And Marie is just as vulnerable right now, we don't want her losin' their baby because of the stress of this whole thing." Sheila remarked then as she grabbed a tissue from the holder on his desk.

"Of course we don't and what we're doin' is helpin' her bear this burden because sometimes when you're in somethin' like this, you don't quite know how to do it by yourself and the Lord doesn't intend it to be that way." Douglas said. "And all of us in here know about the power of prayer and what can happen when you let your faith in God take over." He continued as they began to feel the presence of the Holy Ghost surround them, confirming his words of wisdom and experience. "We all had people prayin' for us when we were out there doin' anything and everything so it's up to us now to pray some fervent effectual prayers so let God use you." He concluded right before he proceeded to lead them in prayer by thanking God for the priviledge of coming boldly to the throne of grace to obtain mercy and grace to help in time of need." It was a prayer for Jerry's protection as well as healing and salvation for the soul.

Within a few minutes of "touching the throne", there was unmistakable confirmation that they had been heard and in God's timing, there would be an answer. Then before leaving the room, he deliberately approached them one by one, petitioning God for their individual situations, problems and issues of this present life.

"The floor nurse told me that he said that he was tired of layin' there hooked up to monitors and tubes and everything else they were doin'." Marie remarked with Donna and Randy. "So he told 'em that he was signin' himself out and nobody could stop him." She added.

"And he's not answerin' his phone huh?" Randy asked her.

She shook her head before speaking. "It's goin' straight to his voicemail." "I've been textin' him and he's not answerin' any of 'em so you know what?"

"What are you thinkin'?" Donna asked as Randy passed Sara over to her.

"I'm at the point where I refuse to let this stress me out because that doesn't do anything but make me feel worse and I can't do that to myself." "I'm givin' it up to God because it's too much for me." She admitted.

"Did they say that he was in any kind of trouble because he's not in the hospital anymore?"

"About all they said was that they weren't responsible for anything that might happen to him because he signed himself out of their care." She said wearily.

"So he probably thought he felt good enough to just walk out of there." Randy said.

"Probably and I know him well enough to realize that he's stubborn and it doesn't matter to him what anybody else thinks." She said shaking her head a little as she suddenly noticed a lengthy text message come through her phone:

"You don't need to try to find out where I am anymore because this is how it ends." "Don't try to make me support a kid that I didn't want in the first place so don't use that as an excuse to keep track of where I am." "If I drop dead somewhere, that's my business so don't worry about it and I'm changing my phone number after this." "I'm out."

"Jesus help me Lord." Marie said quietly as she handed her phone to Donna before slowly standing up. "I'm goin' to bed, that's all I can do right now."…

September 17
Thursday

"This isn't anything new and I can say that because I've been where you are sweetheart." Frances remarked with Marie on Thursday evening out on the deck. "And this doesn't mean that the Lord isn't answerin' prayers either." She continued. "When things don't go the way we want'em to, sometimes we're tempted to think that God has turned His back on us and and a lot of other stuff that the devil will put in your head to throw you off."

"And you know what, that's exactly where I went last night after I finally heard from him." She admitted. "For a minute or two, it was like this isn't happenin' to me but then I thought about the scripture that says not to think things like this are strange?" Is that the way it goes?" She asked her.

"Look that scripture up for me on your phone there and read it to me." "It's in first Peter fourth verse and this is what has gotten me through some times that I can't find the right words for." Frances told her. "It doesn't make sense to our little minds but when you take God at his word, you can't lose." She added right before Marie began reading.

Brethren, think it not strange concerning the fiery trial which is to try you, as though some strange thing happened unto you:.

But rejoice, inasmuch as ye are partakers of Christ's sufferings; that, when his glory shall be revealed, ye may be glad also with exceeding joy.

"What do you get out of that?" Frances asked her with a spirit of love and patience.

"When I read that out loud, it's sayin' to me that I need to be findin' some reasons to be happy through all of this because it's gonna work out for my good." She said, shaking her head a little. "And like you said a minute ago, my mind can't see any good comin' out of this but it's not about what I think or don't think because I don't see the big picture." "And you remind so much of Douglas when I would sit down with him and break things down to him because of the stuff that Irene was puttin' him through." "He was just a few months old in the Lord like you are but when you're fresh out of the world, you have to be nourished like a new baby does and nobody is thinkin' any less of you because of what's goin' on."

She nodded as she silently read the scripture over again to get a better understanding of it. "And I've heard this before at bible classes but it seems different now for some reason."

"It does because you're in a place that you've never been before and it's personal now." Frances told her. "I'm sure you've heard stories from other people that've gone through somethin' like this but it's different when it's you." "But that's when God proves himself to you over and over again and you'll have testimonies that'll stay with you 'til Jesus comes, believe me when I tell you honey."

"And you know what?" She asked her after a moment. "This really shouldn't surprise me that much because things haven't been quite the same since April when I got back to D.C. and tried to explain to him what happened to me." She added as she thought back five months previous.

"And that's to be expected when you're serious about your salvation because it brings about a separation." "And that might've been why William left like he did, he decided one day that he didn't want anything else to do with the Lord or church or any of it." "I got up one mornin' and found an envelope on the kitchen table with three hundred dollars in it and a note was attached to it that told me not to try and find him." She finished as Marie sat shaking her head at the thought.

"And you had four little kids dependin' on you after that."

"Donna was three months old and there I was with nobody but the Lord to take care of us." "I almost panicked but I had just heard a message a couple of weeks before he left and the subject was "Peace in the Fire."

"And you still remember that after all of this time?" Marie asked her, shocked.

"As long as the Lord preserves my mind, I'll never forget it." "And this was long before they were makin' C.D.s and D.V.D.s and downloadin' stuff so you could hear it over and over again."

"It's livestreaming now, you can go back and watch services on your phone or computer." She told her as she tried not to concentrate on Jerry's last communication with her.

"I don't try to keep up with all of that, I just remember havin' a pen and a notebook that I would write scriptures down in and I still have some of 'em packed away somewhere."

"Are you serious?"

"Yes ma'am because it doesn't matter how long ago you heard a word, it never gets old." "Times and people change and I had no idea when the Lord sent that message that it would be a lifeline for me for the next twenty five years."

"Can you remember any of the scriptures from that day?"

"There were three separate ones that I read over and over again until they were a part of me and when you're by yourself at some place and time, just take 'em all in and let God help you understand what He wants from you."

"And my problem is that I'm thinkin' too far ahead of myself." She admitted. I'm havin' these visions of me tryin' to take care of this baby by myself and it's just not a pretty picture."

"So why are you worried about that?" "We're takin' one day at a time because that's all we have." "Yesterday is gone and tomorrow's not promised to us so what's the issue sweetheart?" She asked her as she handed her a napkin from the holder on the table.

"God saw every bit of this comin' and He's not gonna give any more than you can take, do you believe that?"

"You know I do but it helps to hear you say it anyway." She managed to say through her tears. "And I'm so proud of Janice when I think of where she was this time last year and I see how she's handlin' her baby like she's done it all before, it's just mind bogglin' to me."

"And it was the Lord from start to finish and He's not stoppin' with her." "He was orderin' her steps and she had no idea what was goin' on but He's faithful when you trust Him like you never have before."

"I mean she just grew up over night and if it wasn't for Douglas and Chris and James, there's just no tellin' where'd she be."

"So what makes you think you're any different?" "You got yourself together and allowed God to save you and that was just the beginning of what He has in store for you but you have to be proven." "You have to get to the place where you won't let anything or anybody take the peace that God means for you to have, even in a situation like this." She told her. "And I know that your hormones are all over the place right now but pull yourself together and don't let the devil take your mind to places that you shouldn't be."

"Aunt Frances I know you're right and I know that you went through some hard stuff but it'll be a long time before I get where you are." "I'm not lettin' this make me go back to where I was but this is a blow that I didn't see comin." She admitted.

"And most of the time, that's the way it is but the wonderful thing about it, the Lord is in this with you just like He was in the furnace with those boys thousands of years ago." Frances told her. "And if I didn't remember anything else from that message, I never forgot what the man said that night."

"Can you tell me so I won't forget it either?" Marie asked her.

"He said just because God will allow you to be in the fire, He won't let you be consumed by it." She said after a moment.

"It might feel like you are, it might even seem like you've been abandoned by Him but that's exactly how your adversary the devil starts to sift you like wheat and tries to make you feel like God lied to you when His word said He would never leave or forsake you." She said with anointed fervor which caused a powerful reaction between the two of them.

"This is your peace in the fire so don't ever let it go." Frances told her five minutes later as she walked her out to the car. "And whatever you do, stay on your knees because that's where your victory is."…

September 20
Sunday

"I told her I would try to wait 'til she's a week old before I'd come out here and this has been one of the longest seven days I've ever lived through." Michael remarked Sunday afternoon as he helped Chris in the kitchen.

"And she's been so good about gettin' up with her at one and two in the mornin.'" Chris said as she cut watermelon wedges. "I got up with her the night she came home just to check up on her and she was sittin' in the rocker with Kristen cryin' her heart out and I thought somethin' was wrong."

"What was goin' on?" Michael asked, concerned.

"Some of that is post partum stuff goin' on but she said she was thinkin' about how close she had come to gettin' an abortion and she appreciated Douglas so much for tellin' her that wasn't an option." She said after a moment. "It was like she's really overwhelmed at how it's all worked out for her."

"And you don't know thankful I am that it's comin' together for her like it is."

"But you're part of the big picture." "You're most of the reason that she can't believe that this is all happenin' for her."

"I'm just lettin' the Lord help me because when you have so many different things happenin' all at once, it starts to be overwhelming, you know what I mean?" Michael asked her. "And when Marie found out what Jerry's up to, that's when we had to stop talkin' about it and get some serious prayin' done."

"And you can't go by what things look like either." Chris said as she handed him a knife. "What we have to do is get her to realize that this is a test of her faith and she's not in this by herself." She said. "And I'll never forget the day that I ended up on the other side of town at Douglas and Irene's after we had my first sonogram." "I went to pieces because of what they found out that day and I actually had to ask the Lord to forgive me for the way I acted."

"But don't you think that was enough to throw you off?"

"Michael, I didn't have any excuse for the way I reacted to that because I've seen God do too many impossible things." She admitted. "I was so messed up that he wouldn't even let me drive back home and that's when he called James over there and pretty much got us straight."

"I know that feelin' and it doesn't really matter because you know that it's out of love."

"The man does not play." "And I had all these horrible scenarios painted in my head and that wasn't doin' anything but stressin' me out, and God wasn't gettin' any glory out of me actin' like He's an unfit father as mother likes to say."

"They feed off each other don't they?" Michael asked, laughing a little.

"They do and if I don't remember anything else that he told us that day, I'll always remember that he said that we were dealin' with the same God that split the Red sea, what is the problem?"

"And we know about that but sometimes it helps to hear it anyway."

"Of course it does and every time I go in for a check up, they take another look at 'em to make sure that what they found out is really true, they can't believe it." Chris said as she began to think about the powerful testimony that she and James had witnessed.

"So they're not findin' anything else that they can talk about huh?"

"Not a thing because God doesn't do things halfway." Chris said after a moment. "And sometimes we can sit and watch 'em movin' around in there and one is on the left side and the other one's on the right, it's just crazy." She added as she noticed a text from Janice upstairs.

"Can you tell Michael to meet me and Kristen in the family room in five minutes?" "This is it, lol."

"Is this actually happenin' to me?" Michael asked a few minutes later as Janice slowly walked into the room with Kristen, tears coming down her face like a fountain.

"Do you know how great you look right now?" He asked her as he fought his own emotions after seeing her for the first time in a week.

"I tried, Chris had to help me out." She replied as she gingerly sat down next to him and proceeded to confidently pass Kristen over to him.

"She looks like you." He said a few moments later after staring at her, engrossed at what he was simultaneously feeling and seeing.

"That's what everybody says and all of this time I thought she was gonna come out lookin' like Craig." She said, shaking her head a little. "But you can't really go by those sonogram pictures, she doesn't look anything like him anymore."

"Have you heard from Mary Ann since you've been home?"

She shook her head. "After that day in the hospital, she just sort of disappeared but I don't quite trust that."

"But you can't let her take your peace of mind honey." He told her after a moment. "This is the chance for her to see how God has turned this thing around that started out so wrong, into somethin' this beautiful." He said without shame or embarrassment as he gently unwrapped the blanket from around her as his emotions overcame him.

"I don't think I've ever told Douglas how much I appreciate and love him for tellin' me not to do what I was about to." Janice said a couple of minutes later after they both sat in silence, overwhelmed at all that had occurred in just a week's time.

"Then that makes two of us and if you feel like you need to tell him that, then go right ahead." He said as he took a tissue from the holder with his free hand. "And I've had a conversation with him myself because I feel accountable to him when it comes to you." He continued.

She nodded a little with understanding.

"And I want you to tell me if you feel pressured because that's the last thing I wanna do." He said. "But at this point, I think that we need to get a date set to make this altogether right." "I'm ready to be this baby's father and your husband and I can't make it any plainer than that." He finished as he seriously spoke his mind. "James is givin' his guys another month to get done at the house because he knows that I'm not bringin' you home to somethin' half way done."

"Are you serious?" She asked him after a moment. "That quick?"

"Yes ma'am." "They get there around eight or nine after I get home from work and they're workin' hard to get it done" "That's why I really wanted you to see on Sunday what's goin' on with it but stuff happened."

"Stuff did happen but everything worked out anyway." Janice said, trying to alleviate his feelings of responsibility.

"Yeah I have to keep tellin' myself that because it could've been a lot worse." He admitted. "I'm just lettin' God help me."

"It's a little hard to believe but this time last year, we didn't have any idea that our lives would be so different but here we are." Katherine remarked with Michael in the livingroom two hours later." "And it's all because our girl decided to make a bold move but it all worked out for everybody's good." She added as she laid Kristen across her lap.

"So how does it feel to be able to say that you're a grandmother now?"

"So far I'm lovin' it and I thought that it would make me feel old but that's not what I'm gettin' out of this." She said after thinking a moment. "And when I think about how we reacted when she told us that she was pregnant, I get so ashamed of myself." She admitted for the first time to anyone.

"All of us have that feelin' when we think about stuff that happened before God got hold of us." Michael said.

"That's true but what we did affected her to the point where she thought about takin' herself out and that would've been on my conscience for the rest of my life."

"But God had a plan."

"But God had a plan, you're absolutely right." She said, agreeing with him. "And Roy didn't have a problem with it because he knew that she wasn't his and that gave him an excuse to get her out of his house." She said pausing. "And we need to keep all of this real as the young people say and I'm talkin' to you like this because you already know the story." "But just in case somethin' comes up that might make her have some kind of flashback, you'll understand why."

"We've talked about all of that and she told me one day that she's learned how to rebuke stuff like that and keep it movin'." Michael said. "She said that she made the mistake of tellin' one of her co-workers about the bad experiences that she's had with men and she told her that she needs to be gay for the rest of her life." He said, shaking his head.

"And we know where that came from but I'm so thankful for the way Douglas has stepped up and done an amazin' job with her."

"Yeah him and James have been just what she needed to reverse a lot of damage but I'm not so naïve to think that there's not gonna be some stuff that'll come up until she's completely over some issues."

"So do you feel like you love her enough to deal with some problems that're probably gonna come up?" She cautiously asked him.

"You know what?" He began. "I'm not gonna sit here and act like I'm gonna be the perfect husband that won't make mistakes but if I'm doin' it God's way, I can't fail, you know what I mean?" He continued. "I keep goin' over and over that fifth chapter of Ephesians that talks about how to make things work and all I can do to ask the Lord to stand up in me because I already know that there's gonna be stuff to deal with."

"But you feel like you love her enough to overcome all of that?" She asked him again.

"Yes ma'am I do and I'll never forget what James told me one day when we were talkin' about this same thing." He began. "And I know this isn't new or deep but he said that your love type changes the longer that you're together."

"It does and until you go through things together, that's a little hard to understand." "We were married forty years when Roy died and we got through some some hard stuff but we never talked about divorce even though we were separated for a while." "I messed up and did what I did but we worked it out."

"That's not the way most people think anymore but because of what I've seen since I moved here, I know that it can be done."

"Of course it can, and you're unusual because most men wouldn't take on the responsibility of somebody else's child on top of everything else that comes with marriage." Kathryn remarked then.

"That's not gonna stop me from doin' what I know the Lord is givin' me to do." Michael said with conviction. "Somethin' happened with me a couple of weeks ago that I can't forget and it was like God was puttin' a stamp of approval on this and it doesn't matter anymore what other people think about it." He added with an air of confidence.

"That's really good to hear and I'm not doubting anything you're sayin' but I have one thing to say about that."

"I'm listenin' because I need all of the words of wisdom that I can get because I know it's gonna be different from anything I've ever done."

"Whatever you do, please make sure that when she gets old enough to understand, exactly the way she got here." She began. "Don't make the mistake that I did by hiding from Janice who her father was and I paid for it when William came home and told on himself."

"I just happened to be there that day but I had no idea what was goin' on."

"Then you know about what she went through when things came out, and all I'm askin' from you two is not to cover up truth because it has a way of comin' back to haunt you." She said with an air of unmistakable soberness. "And this right here is a little lump of sugar and easy to fall in love with but give her a few years when she starts to grow up." She added. "When she starts to try you with attitude problems etc. etc., you've got to remember this commitment that you're about to make and treat her like she came from you and all of you'll be better off."

"You're tellin' the truth and we'd all be better off if more people would tell it like it is." Michael admitted.

"And it's not because we're better than anybody else but older people like us have been through things and experience is the best teacher."

" That's why I love to hear Aunt Frances talk about stuff and that's because she's been through so much."

"And I've never told her this but maybe I should." Kathryn began as she put Kristen up to her chest. "The day that William came home and let everybody know that he was Janice's father, she called me to make sure he wasn't talkin' out of his head."

"What was that conversation like?" Michael cautiously asked her.

"It was pretty uncomfortable." She said as she thought back. "I had just assumed that it would never come out, Janice was eighteen years old and it was a mistake that both of us made." She freely admitted. "But when she didn't judge me or act like she was ready to chop me to pieces, I was pretty much in shock." She continued as she let a tear come down her face.

"Yeah that wouldn't be her."

"And it was the way that she handled the whole thing that really started my mind to wonder about how she was able to be so gracious about it."

"But you know now don't you?"

"I know now that it wasn't anything but the Lord that was helpin' her that day." "And on top of that, I saw the way that Douglas handled my devilment and I thought to myself, what have they got that I don't?" "I'm goin' to church every Sunday and doin' this and that, what's goin' on?"

"Wow." Michael commented, intrigued with her honesty.

"And then I saw the difference with Janice." She continued. "I was used to her mouthin' off with some major attitude with us and then she comes here and it's like, what did they do with her in a couple of months that I couldn't."

"And that's really hard for me to relate to because by the time I met her, she had already gotten her help." Michael said, laughing a little.

"Excuse me for sayin' this but the girl was a trip and a fall as the kids used to say." "And when I look back on it now, I can understand it a little because she had some anger to deal with and that's how she was handlin' it." "Roy treated her like a dog and whenever I would try to check him about the way he made a difference between her and Marie, he would threaten to come out with it and there I was, pretty much helpless."

"Blackmail in other words."

"That's basically what it was and I after I got that phone call from Frances, I was a little relieved that it had come out." "William told on himself and the rest is history as they say." "He knew he was dyin' and I guess he was gettin' it off of him and if it hadn't been for the way that Douglas and her sisters and Paul embraced her, she might still be dealin' with some serious issues."

"But that's what love does and I realize that things might still trigger some stuff with her but we know where our strength is comin' from too." Michael said after a moment. "And I'm not so naïve to think that there's not gonna be some bumps that we're gonna have to deal with but I've seen since I've been here, that you get through anything when you do it God's way."

"You have some good examples huh?"

"I do, from the time I got here back in April, I made it a point to watch and see what it was that was workin' so well with these guys."

"It works because they know what keeps the peace in a house and like you said, when you do it like God intended, it has to work." "And I don't want you to feel like I'm puttin' you through the third degree because you're marryin' my daughter but I'm really gonna do a lot of prayin' for you two because I know that's what makes the difference." She concluded as Marie walked in then.

"Everything alright?" Michael asked her, reading the expression on her face.

"I really can't believe this but Randy just got a text from Jerry." She began as she sat down next to Kathryn.

"What's goin' on, did he say where he was?"

"He's back in the hospital and he's in Chicago." "He was tryin' to get back to D.C. and he passed out at the airport." She began. "Randy tried to call him and he's not pickin' up so we don't know anything except that he's in a Chicago hospital."

"So I wonder why he got in touch with Randy and didn't call you." Kathryn remarked after thinking for a moment.

"He told me that he was out, which means to me that he's done with me." Marie responded as she managed to keep her composure.

"Don't get too far ahead of yourself." Kathryn said.

"I'm really tryin' not to but whether he likes it or not, he needs a lot of help right now." She said. "But at this point, I'm steppin' back and makin' sure that I keep it together so I won't lose this baby even though he doesn't want anything to do with it."

"How?" Michael asked.

"Michael, I don't get it either." She said. "When I told him I was pregnant, he told me right away to take care of business and get rid of it and those were his exact words."

"Did you tell him that wasn't happenin'?"

"I didn't argue with him because I wasn't gonna start somethin' that wasn't gonna go anywhere." Marie said. "And believe it or not, if this had been this time last year, I might've thought about it but like Douglas told Janice, that's not an option so that's where I am."

"Randy said to meet him and Douglas downstairs in the basement." Michael said then, after receiving a text from him.

"I'll take her, I don't think you're quite ready to take the steps are you?"Marie asked Kathryn as she reached for Kristen.

"Not with a baby in my arms but I'm gettin' there, God is helpin' me." She said a moment later as Michael helped her to stand."I'm on my way."

"Jerry's right around the corner if you wanna put it that way and if he didn't want to be found, he wouldn't have let Randy know where he is." Douglas remarked five minutes later down in the basement office with Terry, Michael, Marie, Sheila and Kathryn. "And Marie, you and your mama weren't with us Tuesday night after you asked us to pray but that's exactly what we did." "We didn't put it off then and we can't now either."

Marie nodded a little in appreciation and agreement with him then.

"And that was some kind of prayer too and evidently, we got through because we know more now than we did then." Sheila said.

"And whatever happens between you two is not really our business but right now, he's pretty sick and he needs our help." Douglas said. "Randy is upstairs tryin' to find out where he is but God knows exactly where he is and when He gets ready for us to know, things will start to happen." He continued. "And just because we don't know where he is, doesn't stop us from doin' what we have to do." He said as they began to respond to the powerful anointing of the Holy Ghost around them before they proceeded to petition the all knowing God in Jerry's behalf.

It was a prayer of thanksgiving and faith that there would be a positive outcome for a difficult situation that could only be resolved by the fervent effectual prayer of the righteous that avail much.

"For with God nothing shall be impossible."

End of Part IV

www.ingramcontent.com/pod-product-compliance
Lightning Source LLC
LaVergne TN
LVHW011710060526
838200LV00051B/2840